"This book calls people to quit—to give up, to surrender, to let go of the actions, attitudes and approaches that have held them back—and to start experiencing all God has for their life and for the life of their church. Get yo[...] read it, and raise up a tribe of quitters."

Mark Batterson, *New York Times* bes[...]
of *The* [...]
lead pastor, National Com[...]

"I love it when someone challenges me to se[...] from a radically different viewpoint. My friend [...] does just that in *Quit Church*. You'll find it c[...] transformational, and after reading this bool[...] church as usual."

Sam Chand, leadership consultant;
author of *Bigger Faster Leadership*

"Every now and again a book comes along that has the potential to revolutionize your life and the life of your church. *Quit Church* is one of those books. It challenges you in six crucial areas to stop doing church as usual and to start pursuing all God has for your future. If you will take the time to read this book and apply the principles that Chris brilliantly lays out, you will find a fresh new perspective and passion for your spiritual journey."

Jamie Stahler, vice president, Outreach, Inc.

"Chris Sonksen is a proven leader and trusted voice who shares powerful wisdom in *Quit Church*. These principles can change your entire experience of God and community. Don't miss this important book!"

Jud Wilhite, author of *Pursued*;
senior pastor, Central Church

"I assume that when you saw the title of this book, you did a double take. And that is exactly what I love about Chris. His insight into leadership and church dynamics is so keen, and his ability to communicate complex truth in an engaging, tangible way can stop you dead in your tracks. Should you really 'quit church'? I'll let you decide, but not until you've dug into this gold mine. You will be surprised at what you read, but in the very best kind of way."

Clayton King, teaching pastor, Newspring Church; author of *Overcome* and *Stronger*

"I love the premise of this book. Right from the introduction, Chris Sonksen reminds us that there's still so much more God has for us. And knowing what to quit is one of the greatest keys to moving into the new thing God has in store. I know this book will be a great win for leaders in all walks of life. It will have a strong impact on the way we serve and love others, too. Get it: get it to your team, get it to your family, and watch what God does through it."

Dino Rizzo, executive director, Association of Related Churches

"Chris's simple and direct approach to this topic has the potential to revolutionize the average churchgoer's experience. This is a must read for every church. It will change your life and the life of your church."

Herbert Cooper, author of *But God*; lead pastor, People's Church

"I never thought I'd endorse the idea of 'quitting church,' until I read Chris Sonksen's intriguing new book, *Quit Church*. This fresh perspective is for everyone who attends church. What would it be like if believers stopped doing church like 'business as usual' and engaged in a way that tapped into the life-changing power and potential of God? Chis takes us through six attitude shifts that can change your life and the life of your church."

Dan Reiland, executive pastor, 12Stone Church

quit
CHURCH

quit
CHURCH

Because Your Life Would Be

Better If You Did

CHRIS SONKSEN

BakerBooks

a division of Baker Publishing Group
Grand Rapids, Michigan

Published by Baker Books
a division of Baker Publishing Group
PO Box 6287, Grand Rapids, MI 49516-6287
www.bakerbooks.com

Printed in the United States of America

ISBN 978-0-8010-9324-1 (pbk.)

Library of Congress Cataloging-in-Publication Data
Names: Sonksen, Chris, 1968– author.
Title: Quit church : because your life would be better if you did / Chris Sonksen.
Description: Grand Rapids : Baker Publishing Group, 2018.
Identifiers: LCCN 2017055469 | ISBN 9780801093241 (pbk.)
Subjects: LCSH: Church renewal. | Habit breaking—Religious aspects—Christianity. | Change (Psychology)—Religious aspects—Christianity. | Church growth.
Classification: LCC BV600.3 .S675 2018 | DDC 248.4—dc23
LC record available at https://lccn.loc.gov/2017055469

18   19   20   21   22   23   24   8   7   6   5   4   3   2

To Dan Reiland. Your leadership and influence have touched thousands of pastors, and I am honored to be one of them. Thank you for the countless hours of phone calls, lunch appointments, email conversations, introductions to other leaders, resources, encouragement, counsel, and guidance that you have graciously and willingly provided throughout the years. Whatever I put my hand to has your fingerprints all over it. I am eternally grateful to call you my coach and friend.

CONTENTS

FOREWORD

Dave Ferguson

Behind every "no" from God is a greater "yes!" A mentor of mine would remind me to reflect on that truth as I was preparing to teach. His point was that God doesn't just say "no" to selfishness, for example; he also offers us the great "yes!" of generosity. God doesn't create an arbitrary boundary by saying "no" to sex outside of marriage; he offers us the greater "yes!" of intimacy. And God doesn't just say "no" to anxious living; he says "yes!" to a life where he is Lord of all. "Behind every 'no' from God is a greater 'yes!'"—this truth has revolutionized my thinking and teaching.

In *Quit Church* Chris Sonksen will revolutionize your spiritual life and your church. Chris brilliantly applies my mentor's truism by challenging us to say "no" to unhealthy spiritual practices so we can experience God's greater "yes!" Chris Sonksen is someone you should listen to. He leads a great church. Chris coaches hundreds of church leaders across the country, and he is a constant learner and a thought leader when it comes to church life. Read and learn!

Russ quit church. Here is his true story.

Russ came to church on Saturday nights. He would always sit on the outside aisle so he could leave in the middle of the service to call the local golf course as soon as Sunday tee times became available. Russ had no real interest in getting to know anyone at church. He primarily showed up to keep his wife happy (and thus himself!). Tithing was not even a consideration for Russ, but he would throw in a few bucks to make sure he covered his own cost. His serving was limited to occasionally helping with the hospitality ministry, but only during the service he attended. Russ couldn't imagine more than one hour a week at church. Then came the Saturday night when they said something at church that pushed him beyond his comfort level and Russ told his wife they needed to find another church. So Russ left that church and took his same half-hearted spiritual routine to the church across town.

Ten years later, Russ is not only back at his old church; but he has returned with a new set of spiritual practices. Russ is on staff and oversees one of their campuses. Russ leads a small group. He is also one of the most generous people you will ever meet. Russ serves both when he's on the clock and when he's off the clock. Russ is a raving fan of the mission of Jesus!

What happened? Russ had a life-changing encounter with Jesus, and in Chris Sonksen's words, Russ quit church!

So try quitting church! This book wants the same life-changing transformation that Russ experienced for you and everyone in your church! *Quit Church* will challenge you personally and your church corporately to quit the same old routine of nominalism and to experience a brand-new set of spiritual practices. If you want a life-changing experience like Russ, then read *Quit Church* and do what it says! If you want the people in your church to have transformational encounters with Jesus, read *Quit Church* and do what it says!

Now turn the page, start reading, and remember, behind every "no" from God is a greater "yes!"

INTRODUCTION

Just Quit Already

It's late Tuesday afternoon, and my plane has just touched down in Dallas, Texas. I've got a very short window to exit the plane, board the tram, and get to my next gate. And of course I'm sitting in the twenty-first row, which makes the exit process even longer. As the plane reaches the gate, the "Fasten Seat Belt" sign turns off, and the race begins. I guess it's not really a race; it's more of a hurry-up-and-wait. Have you ever noticed that when you're in a hurry, no one else is? That's exactly how I feel. I am standing there watching people take their time getting out of their seats and removing their luggage from the overhead compartment, all the while continuing to chitchat with their neighbors and stroll ever so slowly off the plane. I'm a Christian and a pastor, so I keep a Christlike smile on my face the whole time, but in my mind I'm letting them have it. After what seems like an eternity, it is my turn to exit. I grab my luggage and rush off the plane.

I quickly move down the hallway into the concourse. Having not planned well, I am wearing flip-flops, and as I'm running, they are falling off my feet. I hurry up the escalator and rush to the tram, which will take me to the proper terminal for my final flight home. I time it perfectly. I arrive at the exact moment the tram doors are shutting, and I just make it on. As we proceed down the track, I look up at the map and discover that my destination is four stops away. Now my Christlike patience is really being tested. Each of the stops seems to take forever, and once again no one seems to be in a hurry except me. I feel like I am on a ride at Disneyland: everybody's happy, smiling, and taking their time. The tram finally arrives at my stop. I rush through the exit doors and head to the escalator, which takes me down to the concourse. With one flip-flop on my foot and one in my hand, I arrive at the gate—only to discover there has been a two-hour delay. I could've looked at the app on my phone or the fifty departure monitors that I ran past to see whether the plane was on time, but this isn't the day for common sense.

As I'm standing there catching my breath, I hear a voice call out, "Chris." I turn around and see a buddy of mine whom I haven't seen in quite some time. He too is a pastor, and, like me, he travels a lot. He says to me, "Are you on this flight too?" I nod my head to indicate that I am. We begin to talk a bit about where we flew in from and what we were doing there, which leads us into a brief update on each other's life. After a few minutes of chatting, he says to me, "Let's go to the Admirals Club Lounge, and we can hang out there."

Keep in mind that I have been traveling for years. I look at my friend with a little confusion and say, "Admirals Club Lounge—we can't go in there; it's only for pilots."

He looks at me as if I am joking. "What are you talking about?"

I point at the door directly across from us that says ADMI-
RALS CLUB LOUNGE. "How can you get in there?" I ask. "Isn't
that where pilots hang out before their next flight?"

He finally realizes that I am serious—and the laughter
begins. He barely manages to get out the next sentence amid
all his laughing. "All these years traveling and you have no
idea what the Admirals Club Lounge is? That is hilarious.
It's not a place for pilots; it's a place for people who travel a
lot. It's like a little club with seating areas and restaurants,
and some of them even have a gym inside."

"Are you serious?" I respond.

He says, or actually sort of laughs out the words, "Come
on." We walk across the hallway, push the button on the wall,
wait for the doors to slide open, and walk in.

He presents his ID and a card, and the next thing I know
we are headed up in an elevator to the Admirals Club Lounge.
As the elevator doors open, everything changes. Downstairs
in the terminal, there are thousands of people rushing down
the hallways; it's packed, difficult to find a seat, and very
noisy. But the lounge is quiet and peaceful. People are seated
in soft, cushioned chairs snacking, having lunch, doing a
little work, watching TV. It is amazing. There is even a quiet
room where you can lay on stretched-out chairs and take
a nap. Unbelievable! I had no idea this place existed, and
it is a thousand times better than sitting in the terminal
area.

But you know what is even crazier than all of this? When
my friend presents his ID and card at the front desk, they
ask for my ID as well. When I hand it over, the lady behind
the counter says, "Mr. Sonksen, you're already a member."

"What?"

"You have been a member for a few years now, but you never activated your card." She explains, "Sometimes airlines will give you a membership if you earn enough miles, and you have had enough so that you have had access to the Admirals Club Lounge for several years. All you had to do was walk through the doors."

All these years I had access to something better, and I didn't even know it. All these years I had the wrong mind-set about the Admirals Club. I thought it was for other people and not for me. I didn't think it was something that I could access or enjoy. I had a complete misunderstanding and didn't realize that I had the right to be in there too. For years I sat in plastic chairs in crowded and noisy terminals, not even realizing that just a few feet away was a door that would lead me to something so much better. But I never walked through it. How crazy and sad is that?

I see the same crazy and sad problem existing in the local church. As I travel across the nation coaching pastors and speaking in churches, I find that the same misguided mind-set that I had about the Admirals Club Lounge is present among Christians. We miss out on so much that has been promised to us by God. We sit in the terminal of our own life, accepting much less than is available to us.

There are over three thousand promises from God in the Bible. Many of these promises are unconditional, like God's love—no matter what we do, he is going to keep loving us. He is always faithful, and his love never ends. However, there are conditional promises as well. These are promises where God says, "If you do this, then I'll do that." These conditional promises cover areas that God wants to bless us in, such as joy, peace, love, finances, success, and many other areas that we all want more of in our life. All of this is available to each and every one of us. Like the Admirals Club Lounge, the door to all that God has for your life is only a few feet away. God is looking to shower you with his presence and promises.

So if God is looking to bless your life in ways that you have only imagined, what is holding you back from getting that blessing? Why are you sitting in a terminal when God has invited you to the lounge? Jeremiah 29:11 says, "'For I know the plans I have for you,' declares the LORD, 'plans to prosper you'" (NIV). So if he is the one inviting you to the lounge, what is keeping you on the outside? Two things, really.

Your Approach

You're going at this all wrong.

God is in love with you and wants to bless your life in more ways than you could possibly imagine, but when it comes to the conditional promises, there is a role that you and I must play. We have to realize that when it comes to these types of promises, God responds to our actions. For example, we love the portion of Malachi where the Lord says, "I will open the windows of heaven for you. I will pour out a blessing so great you won't have enough room to take it in!" (3:10). That sounds amazing! Where do we sign up for that? We love the word picture of heaven opening up and us receiving a blessing so big that it overflows. Who wouldn't want that?

But it's the first part of that verse that many people don't embrace—the part where God says to "bring all the tithes into the storehouse." God is very straightforward about this. *You give to me a percentage of your income, and I'll bless you big.* But we want the promises without paying the price.

19

We won't give up what's in our hands, but we want God to give up what's in his.

We will talk more about giving and generosity in a later chapter, but I wanted to give this small example to you in order to get you thinking about the noncommittal, casual approach we often take to God and to church. This casual approach to commitment is embedded in us and, quite honestly, hard to escape. Think about how many options you have when you turn on your TV. Or when you quickly flip through social media, if you don't like one story, you go on to the next. The same is true on the web. So many stories, ideas, advertisements, and so on are being thrown at you, and whatever you don't like you just ignore. It happens in relationships too. If you don't like it, go on to the next one.

> We won't give up what's in our hands, but we want God to give up what's in his.

This type of culture has bled into our faith. Maybe we didn't mean for it to, but it has. We approach our Christianity with a casual commitment to the things that God has called us to do and be. Studies done by *Relevant* magazine showed that in some churches, as few as 10 percent of members tithe.[1] Barna research discovered that only 52 percent of Christians have shared their faith in the last twelve months.[2] Even when it comes to our commitment to the local church, if we don't like something or if something doesn't go our way, then fine, we'll go to another church. The virtue of loyalty is thrown out the window on account of our preference.

Again, we want all of the incredible blessings of God, we want him to pour out from the windows of heaven and shower us with his goodness, but we don't want to live up to our side of the deal. Meanwhile, God isn't desiring to hold anything back from us. He's not in heaven hoping we'll mess up so that he doesn't have to bless us. As a matter of fact, it is completely the opposite. As Proverbs 13:21 teaches us, "Blessings chase the righteous" (TLB). He's on the search for those he can bless.

Remember, we are not speaking of unconditional promises, such as God's love. We are talking about the types of both blessing and reward that God is eager to give to those who fulfill their part of the bargain. By neglecting these things, we are leaving so much on the table. So many promises, rewards, blessings, and favors are never cashed in because of the casual-commitment approach we have come to accept.

As this book unfolds, I will show you how our addiction to a casual-commitment approach affects almost every area of our lives: volunteering, discipleship, relationships with each other, commitment to the local church, and reaching the lost, among others. At first glance, these may seem like fairly general topics in the church world, but understand that when put into practice, they carry with them a promise of great blessing from our Creator.

In all these areas, God wants more from us, but that is only because he has more for us.

Your View

Not only is your approach off, your whole perspective needs to change.

Have you ever said to yourself, *I need to get in shape.* Maybe you saw an ad in a magazine with someone who had six-pack abs and thought, *I can do that.* So you got all inspired and headed down to the local gym. A rep gave you the standard tour, showing you all the amenities. At the end of the tour, the rep gave you a few payment options and tried to upsell you on time with a personal trainer.

Now let's say you went for the full package, trainer and all. You set your first appointment to meet with the trainer on Monday morning. (It has to be a Monday, because that's when all new fitness regimes start.) Now the work really begins. I know a little about this process, because I have a few friends who are trainers, and they will all tell you the same thing: They cannot force you to work out. They cannot follow you around and make sure you eat right. They can give you a great workout plan and map out the type of meals you need to have and how often you need to eat, but you are the one who has to follow through. You are the one who has to carry out the right activities. They'll point you in the right direction and give you all the tools you need, but in the end, your actions will shape your results.

It is up to you to make it happen. It's up to you to stay motivated and on course. To think anything less would be a mistake. To blame the trainer because you didn't get the results you want would be foolish. But we often take this unhealthy view and transport it into our church life. We don't say it out loud or ever express it to anyone, but we feel that it is the responsibility of the pastor to motivate us, inspire us, or instill enough passion in us to get us to follow the biblical principles that God says, when followed, will reap a great reward.

I travel all across the nation, and I see firsthand pastors and leaders who are struggling to develop a creative approach that will move their congregation to begin taking action on a principle that God taught thousands of years ago. They hold a giving challenge with a money-back guarantee so that people will try tithing for a period of time; or they give a prize away to those who invite the most people to church; or they give people a chance to volunteer with little to no commitment in a desperate hope that the people will like it and want to continue.

Now please hear me. I am *not* saying that this is wrong. As a matter of fact, we've tried a crazy amount of these things in our church and will continue to do so. We want to do whatever it takes to help people follow Jesus and to receive all that he has for their lives. But pastors shouldn't have to resort to these pleas, at least not to those who already consider themselves believers. It is not the job of the pastor to keep us spiritually fit seven days a week. The pastor teaches, instructs, and points the way, but it's our job to carry it out.

If you are a Christian, things like giving, serving, inviting, being loyal, and other behaviors that will be tackled in this book should be a part of your life. But, perhaps unintentionally, you are waiting for the pastor to come up with the right gimmick, preach the right message, share the right Scripture passage, show the right video, or drop the right catchphrase that will somehow spark enough passion in you to finally act on God's Word.

So because you don't have the passion or because you haven't been inspired, you simply stay on the sideline. You imagine that you'll take action when you feel inspired. But that is not how it works. Consider a marriage. If you think *I am only going to show love when I am passionate,* then you are going to have a troubled marriage. You practice love and kindness in your marriage even when you don't feel like it. You take action and the passion follows.

23

The same is true with spiritual practices. You don't wait to feel passion before you begin. You do the practices first, and the passion will follow. Taking it a step further, you do the practices even if the passion doesn't follow for a long time. That's called commitment. You don't always feel like doing the right thing in your marriage, but you do it anyway—or at least you should. In the same manner, you may not always feel like doing the right thing in your spiritual life, but you do it anyway.

Winning Starts with Quitting

Changing your approach and adjusting your perspective is not as difficult as you might think. In fact, it's more about just quitting.

Yes, quitting.

I have read countless motivational books and have seen thousands of motivational quotes on social media. They all encourage you to keep going, don't give up, never stop, stay persistent, run your race, no excuses, get it done, and a thousand other ways of saying that if you want to win, you can't quit. Now I love motivational books—as a matter of fact I have written motivational books—but today I am inviting you to embrace a word that you won't hear me say often: *quit.*

The only way you can win in the spiritual life is to quit. The only way to inherit the conditional promises, covenants, blessings, and rewards that God is eager to give you is to quit. In this case, quitting is not the problem; it is the solution.

Quitting is part of being successful. For some of you, this is music to your ears. "You're telling me that all I have to do

24

to win and be successful is to quit? I can do that!" Before you start jumping up and clicking your heels together, you have to see the full picture. Yes, quitting is easy, and in our culture it is done quite frequently. We quit school, marriages, businesses, gym memberships—all sorts of things. But the type of quitting we will be talking about is different. It's quitting the attitudes and approaches that are holding you down. It's quitting to think and act in ways that keep you and your church from winning. It reminds me of Hebrews 12:1, which says, "Let us strip off every weight that slows us down, especially the sin that so easily trips us up." If you don't learn to quit some of the ways you have been approaching the promises of God and start changing some of the attitudes you have displayed in the church that you attend, you will lose, the body of Christ will lose, and you will miss out on everything God has for you. Success starts with quitting.

> Quitting is not the problem; it is the solution.

This is true not only for your church life but for almost anything else worth pursuing in life. If you want to earn a degree, you will have to quit spending time doing other things so that you can focus on your schooling. If you want to lose weight, you will have to quit your poor eating habits. If you want to save money, you will have to quit your poor spending habits. In many cases, the only way to win is to quit. It's true in athletics, in business, in your personal life, and definitely in your spiritual life. If you want to win, you have to quit. In the next several chapters, we will dive into all kinds of quitting opportunities in greater detail, but it's important that right now, before you continue any further in this book, you come to realize that if you want to win, you must quit.

25

How You Win

As we move through this book, you will see how, if you will quit the areas that you will be challenged in, you will win. When I say win, I mean you will win God-style. You are his child, and he is in love with you. Jesus left heaven and came to earth for you. He crossed the galaxies just to have a relationship with you. The God who does all of that wants to bless your life. Remember, there are promises and covenants that he makes with you and me.

God wants to shower you with his goodness. He wants you to win in your relationships, finances, and future. Hebrews 11:6 teaches that "he rewards those who sincerely seek him." God has no desire to hold back his hand of favor on your life. That's why if you will quit and give up the casual approach to the spiritual practices that we will look at in this book, you will release the promises that have been given to you in Scripture. God is ready to release them if you are ready to quit. He rewards those who seek him. It's a promise from God, and he never goes back on his promises.

As we go forward together, I want you to know that I write from a place of deep conviction and a desire for you to become and to receive all that God has for you. I travel throughout the nation and meet hundreds of Christians who are defeated. I can see it in their eyes. They don't feel like they are winning in life. Some of them have relationships that are in turmoil. For some, their finances are a mess, and they are neck-deep in debt. Some of them are being robbed of joy and peace.

And to be quite honest with you, I am tired of it. I can't stand seeing God's people walking, talking, speaking, and acting as if they are second-class citizens in his kingdom.

This is not God's intent for our lives. We are made to be more than conquerors in Christ Jesus. That's my heart behind all of this: I want to see victory in every area of your life, and I am 100 percent confident it can happen for you if you quit.

How Your Church Wins

The church is the bride of Christ and is described as spotless (Eph. 5:27). Think about that for a moment: we are his bride. A bride is to be taken care of, her needs are to be met, and she is to be defended against any attackers. The first local church mentioned in the New Testament was a church that loved each other, encouraged each other, and gave generously. They worshiped together and met each other's needs, and the Bible says they grew daily.

Jesus wants his bride to thrive: to have the money to grow, to invest in the community, to bring compassion to the world, to have people serving and volunteering in areas that minister to others as well as bring fulfillment and purpose to the person serving. He wants his people to be in authentic and genuine relationships with each other; to defend each other, not to attack each other; to show love and encouragement to pastors, to leaders, and to the entire body of Christ; to refuse to gossip, post negative messages on social media, or blast the church because something didn't go our way. This is the kind of bride Jesus wants. This is the kind of church and people he wants to bless. He is looking for it, and his hand is ready to shower you and the church you attend with more of his favor than you could possibly imagine. But it all starts when you decide with everything inside of you to simply quit.

one

Quit Expecting
to Wake Up in Heaven

It was about 11:45 p.m., and my plane had landed in Seattle. I was definitely tired from a full day of traveling. I grabbed my belongings and headed through the terminal to the ground-transportation area. I was going to catch the shuttle that would take me to my hotel. As the doors opened up, I was hit by the extremely cold weather that only January could provide. I have lived in Southern California my whole life, so any time it drops below fifty degrees, I think hypothermia is going to kick in. One of the airport employees told me that it was nineteen degrees. That may feel normal to you, but it is anything but normal for me.

I found my way to the shuttle area, and there was one other gentleman standing there. I put my bags down and started to walk around a bit to keep warm. Several minutes went by, and still no shuttle. The man who was waiting with me was clearly getting more and more frustrated. He never said anything to me directly, but under his breath he was mumbling a variety of phrases that can't be repeated in this book. He was upset that it was cold and that we had been waiting now for quite some time.

After about fifteen minutes the shuttle arrived. The driver jumped out of the vehicle and quickly apologized for his delay. He shared that there had been a problem with his last vehicle and he had to get another one from the hotel. This man's apology was genuine and heartfelt, but it made no difference to the man who was waiting with me. He complained to the driver about the weather, his long day and the amount of time he had had to wait. The driver continued to apologize and never lost his cool, but that didn't make any difference to this man. He clearly wasn't happy. We boarded the shuttle and drove to the hotel. The man still had a few more comments as we made our way down the road. As we exited the shuttle, I kindly let the irritated man go in front of me—partially because he was already upset and I didn't want to aggravate him anymore, and partially because he was bigger than I was and I didn't want to get hurt.

The person behind the hotel counter began to check him in. The man proceeded to tell the clerk how frustrated he was, how long he had had to wait, how long of a day he had had, and how bad the weather was. The person behind the counter did a great job keeping a smile on her face and apologizing for any inconvenience the hotel had caused. After a few signatures (and several complaints), the man received the key to his room and was told by the woman at the counter that when he got off the elevator his room would be immediately to the right. The man looked at her with frustration, and I knew exactly what was about to happen. He said, "Are you telling me this room is next to the elevator?"

She responded, "Yes. Is that a problem?"

The man's voice raised as he said, "Yeah, it's a problem. I don't want to be next to the elevator. I won't be able to sleep hearing that thing go up and down all night. Put me in another room."

She explained, "I'm sorry sir but that is the only room we have available." He went ballistic. He told her that he had frequented this hotel chain often and that he should be taken care of above anyone else. He also rehashed the same story that I had now heard three times. He complained about the kind of day he had had, the long travel, the waiting for the shuttle, the weather—and now he railed at her about the room next to the elevator. Although he went off for a while, she continued to say, "I'm sorry sir, we don't have any other rooms available. This is all we have for you." I was standing behind the man waiting my turn, but I must say, I was thinking to myself, *If you don't have any other rooms, what's going to happen to me?* The man grabbed his things, mumbled, complained, and rushed off down the hallway, stating that he was going to speak to the management and that he would never come back to this hotel.

I approached the counter and said to the clerk, "You are doing a great job. I know sometimes things can be tough when it comes to customer service, but you are doing awesome and handling everything so well."

She put the biggest smile on her face and said to me, "Thank you so much. I really needed to hear that."

I gave her my name and my credit card and told her I was checking in. I must admit I was still wondering if there was a

31

room for me. She started looking at her computer screen and said to me, "We are all sold out. Somehow we overbooked. I am really sorry about this, but I guess I will just have to put you in a suite."

This of course put a big smile on my face. Instead of being next to the elevator like the other guy, I was booked into a suite. I have no idea why she didn't offer the other man a suite—maybe it was because of his attitude—but nonetheless I was happy to receive these wonderful accommodations.

What does this story about the man with the bad attitude have to do with this chapter? Well, if we're honest, we will all admit to having a similar demeanor when we walk through church doors on any given Sunday morning. We get frustrated by something we don't like, and we may even share it with other people, oftentimes completely ignoring the damage we are causing to both believers and nonbelievers. In doing so, we create tension and disunity in the church body. The end result is that the kingdom of God loses. And we lose too.

Why Do People Get Frustrated with Their Church?

The reasons for people's frustration in a church vary. Maybe they are upset because of a style change in the church. Maybe a certain program they love and believe in has ended. Maybe they feel like the decisions being made about finances are not the decisions they would make if they were in charge. Maybe they see a change in leadership that they don't agree with or don't understand. Maybe the methods are different than what they would choose. Maybe the church is putting a stronger emphasis on outreach, and in their opinion ignoring discipleship. This list isn't exhaustive. Not always seeing eye to eye is normal. Having different opinions is normal. But what is sad and breaks the heart of God is that many individuals who get frustrated or leave the church respond in an unloving and ungodly manner, and it creates a chain of negative results.

Where does all of this frustration come from? I believe James 4:1–2 gives us insight about where this problem stems from: "What is causing the quarrels and fights among you? Don't they come from the evil desires at war within you? You want what you don't have." Isn't that really the problem? We want our way, and when we don't get it, we get upset. Whether it's the man at the hotel or you in the church you attend, if we don't get our way, we get upset. Many of us create a lot of pain, heartache, and damage to the kingdom of God.

A good friend who is pastor of a large church in Asia once told me, "I would never want to pastor in America. The people of your country have no idea what loyalty is." He went on to say, "The people in my country don't leave a church simply because they get upset or because they don't like something. They work it out and talk it out, but they don't abandon their spiritual family. We are loyal to Jesus and loyal to our church family."

Loyalty in America runs paper-thin. One of the reasons for this problem is the wide variety of choices we have. This get-what-you-want-when-you-want-it system has bled into other areas of our lives, including our church life. If we aren't happy with something in the church, or if something doesn't go our way, we simply wander down the street to the next church or isolate ourselves from relationships and watch our favorite church online. The only problem with this solution is that as soon as the new pastor or church doesn't live up to our expectations or do things the way we think they should be done, we head off to the next church.

Your Church Will Never Be Perfect

Let me clarify some misunderstandings you may have about your church. It isn't perfect. Your pastor isn't perfect. The leadership isn't perfect. The people who attend, and that includes you, aren't perfect. Nothing is perfect about your church except Jesus. So because no one in your church is perfect and it is made up of imperfect people, there are and always will be problems. As I always say, "If you find the perfect church, don't go there, because once you do, it won't be perfect anymore." Yes, it is sarcastic, but it is nevertheless true. None of us, including and especially me, is perfect. This chapter is titled "Quit Expecting to Wake Up in Heaven" because your church isn't heaven. Quit looking for the perfect church; it isn't out there.

We are called to give our heart, prayer, love, support, faithfulness, loyalty, encouraging words, and positive attitude to the church that God has us at. There may be times when someone you know in the church starts to complain or become negative. When that happens, just remember that you are not responsible for other people's responses; you are responsible only for your own. You do what is pleasing in the sight of God when it comes to your church, and the rest is in his hands.

I am not saying that no matter what happens, stay in the church and keep supporting it. There are some rare occasions when exiting (without talking to everyone about it) may be the right thing to do. But in my experience, leaving should be the exception and not the rule. It should never be our initial response. Too many people, when things don't go their way, respond with negative words and painful reactions, and ultimately abandon their spiritual families. This is not what God intended for his bride. God's desire for the local church is that we operate in a spirit of unity and love; that we are faithful to each other, encourage each other, and believe the best about each other; that we speak words of life to each other and about each other.

> You are not responsible for other people's responses; you are responsible only for your own.

Again, your church isn't perfect. No church is perfect. The imperfection found in all of us can create tension. How do we handle it? How does God want us to operate and function in his body of believers called the church? God loves his church and every person who attends it. He wants us to have healthy relationships with each other, to act and react in a healthy and godly manner, and to be a family that he can be proud of and that people on the outside want to be a part of. This is the kind of family God wants. This is the way he wants us to be with each other.

Mark 3 shows both confusion and dissension among the religious people and the crowds that were following Jesus. Jesus said to them, "If a kingdom is divided against itself, that kingdom cannot stand" (v. 24 NIV). The heart of Jesus shines through in his statement to these people and still rings loud to us in our generation. He wants us to love each other, not to argue with each other; to build each other up, not to tear each other down; to encourage each other, not to

35

discourage each other; to support the pastor, leaders, and members of the church we attend, not to look for something to criticize or belittle—actions that hurt the body of Christ and hurt Christ himself.

I remember being in a grocery store years ago. I was standing in line behind a lady who had two children with her. The children were acting in a way that clearly displeased the mom. They were fighting with each other and pushing each other, and when the mom tried to intervene, they disrespected her authority. As I stood behind her watching all of this happen, the mom suddenly leaned down and forcefully whispered: "Stop acting this way. You're embarrassing me." Instantly, God spoke to my heart about his church; about me and you and the way we sometimes treat the pastor and leaders when we don't get our way; about how we respond when a decision is made that we wouldn't make if we were in charge; about the words we say, who we say them to, and how we say them; about how we manage to justify our attitude and behavior when clearly it goes against his Word. I felt like God spoke to me in that grocery store line and said, "How this mom is feeling right now with her misbehaving children is how my children make me feel at times." At that moment I wondered if God had ever thought that about me. Had I ever acted like a child?

I ask you the same question today. Has God ever thought that about you? Has God ever watched you act in ways toward your church or leadership that were displeasing to him, or heard you say things that were hurtful to other people in the body of Christ, and wanted to lean down and whisper in your ear, "Stop doing that"?

Loyalty Is a Personal Choice, but It's Never Personal

We are big on personal choices in our society. You can do whatever you want and be whatever you want; it's your choice. Although I agree that it is your personal choice to do what you want, you have to realize that a personal choice is never personal. It always affects people, and usually it's those you love the most. For instance, if you have a family and you make a personal choice to overspend or mismanage your funds, that was your personal choice, but it's not just personal. It will affect other people. You can make a choice about your health and do whatever you want; it's your personal choice. But make no mistake, your personal choice is never personal. It affects other people. Even in the church, you can choose to act in a way that doesn't show love or loyalty, but understand that your personal choice is never personal. People will get hurt.

When it comes to the subject of you and me exercising loyalty, God has plenty to say. Over eight thousand times in the Bible the concept of loyalty is referred to: loyalty to God, loyalty to each other, loyalty to authority, loyalty to family, loyalty to friends, the results of disloyalty, and the loyalty with which God makes covenants. This subject is referred to more times than heaven and hell combined. God clearly has a heart for this area of our life. Over and

> Although loyalty runs thin in our culture, it doesn't run thin in the heart of God.

over the Bible communicates the kind of loyalty that God looks for in us. Although loyalty runs thin in our culture, it doesn't run thin in the heart of God.

The kind of loyalty God looks for shows up among his people in many ways:

- Supporting, resourcing, and championing the mission of God (Prov. 3:9–10)

- Standing strong during difficulty rather than looking for the exit door (Eccles. 4:12)

- Choosing to speak only what is helpful and honoring (Eph. 4:29)

- Praying for our pastors and leaders every day (1 Tim. 2:1–2)

- Focusing on the good rather than the bad (Phil. 4:8)

- Being careful not to criticize or judge (Matt. 7:1–5)

- Choosing not to listen to or spread gossip (Ps. 141:3–4; Prov. 16:28)

- Guarding our heart and attitude (Prov. 4:23)

- Making sure the pastor feels honored, not just tolerated (1 Thess. 5:12–13)

- Stopping those who verbally attack our church and its leaders (Titus 3:10)

When we exercise this kind of loyalty, God is honored. When we choose to live this way, we are choosing to be like Christ. We are modeling his word and character. This is what builds the church. This is what builds the kingdom of God. This is what brings honor to his name. This is what Jesus was talking about when he said, "By this everyone will know that you are my disciples, if you love one another" (John 13:35 NIV). This kind of loyalty is what others need to see in us. It's what our kids need to see in us. As I've said, loyalty is a personal choice, but it's never personal. It always affects other people.

Attack the Problem, Not the Person

There are going to be times when you don't like something at the church you attend or you don't fully agree with how something is being run. There is no way of getting around that. We are different people with different opinions. Tension may arise in many areas.

Church matters—You may disagree about programs that end, budget decisions, staff changes, building projects, relocations, operations, fund-raising choices, politics, or missions.

Spiritual matters—You may disagree with how the church is addressing discipleship programs, prayer times, sermon presentations, communion, worship, or fasting or, my all-time favorite, you may think that "the church isn't deep enough."

Personal matters—You may have been hurt or offended due to personal attention you never received from the church, whether hospital visits, home visits, returned phone calls, returned emails, or someone noticing that you have been absent.

The question isn't whether the pastors, leadership, or church is going to let you down. The question is how you are going to respond when they inevitably do. I say inevitably because, once again, the church is made up of imperfect people, so it will never be perfect, just like you're not perfect. Because it's not perfect, you will be let down, and your response when you are let down will reveal the type of character and integrity you have. It's said that character is made in crisis; but I think it

39

is *displayed* in crisis. It's easy to be kind and gracious when everything is going your way, but what are you like when things aren't going your way? That will show more about you than almost anything else.

> It's easy to be kind and gracious when everything is going your way, but what are you like when things aren't going your way?

My advice to you is simple. Follow the principles Jesus taught in Matthew 18. If you have a problem with another person, go to them at once. Jesus doesn't encourage you to go to three or four other people in the church and then go to the person. He says to go to that person at once. Talk with them and share your concerns. Work it out with that person. Also, he doesn't say to run to social media to post your disappointment or concern about the church or its leaders. That is absolutely inappropriate and spiritually wrong. That creates damage for the church and for the kingdom of God. It hurts the pastor, it hurts fellow believers, and it gives nonbelievers yet another reason not to go to church. Stop doing these things. You are causing so much irrevocable damage. Just follow the biblical principles Jesus laid out by going to your brother or sister at once.

Please note that even if you share your concerns with the pastor or a staff member, things might not change. Leaders may feel that the choice they are making is the right choice, and they may feel led by God to move in that direction. Your duty is to respect and honor the authority that God has given them and to support and champion the vision of the church. However, if they blatantly and consciously go against God's Word, ask you to be a part of something immoral, or ask you to sell all you have, shave your head, and live in a compound, then of course you can't keep walking on the journey with them. Ninety-nine percent of the time, though, that is not the problem. If there is tension, most of the time it will come from a difference of opinion. When that happens, respond right. Keep your heart right. If it needs to be addressed, then follow the biblical guidelines. Anything less will create damage and will ultimately reveal your true character.

How You Win

When you choose to quit responding in the way that has become normal for society and, unfortunately, normal for the church, you will win. If you quit thinking that the pastor, church, and leaders are perfect and stop holding them to a standard that you can't even live up to, then you will win. If you quit running to others and running to social media when you are hurt or disagree with something in the church, you will win. Once you quit doing these things and you start to operate in a spirit of loyalty, you will win.

Why will you win? Because God promises that you will. Proverbs 21:21 says, "He who pursues righteousness and loyalty / Finds life, righteousness and honor" (NASB). You win when you pursue loyalty, when you seek to act and react in a way that is pleasing to God. It keeps your heart clean and your attitude in the right place. It models a Christlike spirit to those who are watching you. To the people in your church, it shows you can be counted on. To the nonbelievers in your life, it shows that love and integrity exist inside the local church. To your children, it displays the kind of loyalty you want them to show in their future marriage, job, or church.

41

The Bible promises that you will receive honor when you show loyalty. It's simple: you win, the people around you win, and God wins when you show loyalty.

How Your Church Wins

There are so many ways that your church wins when you operate in a spirit of loyalty and unity, when you refuse to gossip, judge, criticize, or speak negatively. Think about some of the great things that can happen for your church when you are loyal:

- The pastor doesn't have to go through the unnecessary hurt and heartache that is created by negative people.
- The pastor's kids have a greater chance of being healthy believers as they grow up, because they will view the church as something great to belong to rather than something that has brought their parents pain.
- The church shines brightly in the community, because there isn't the ugly stigma of indifference surrounding it.
- The people center more on loving one another than hurting one another.
- The leadership can focus on building the strategy of the church rather than dealing with the behaviors of the church.
- The church stands stronger, more unified, and more aligned.
- The church can expect even greater things from God, because God knows he can trust the people of that church.

There are so many items in the win column when we behave in a Christlike manner in our local church.

As we close this chapter, please remember that your church isn't perfect, and it never will be, so quit expecting this will magically happen. Choose to speak what is good and healthy. Choose to believe the best, not the worst. Cheer your pastor on, support the leadership, and love your spiritual family. This is what God wants from each of us, and when we do it, we win and our church wins.

Questions for Study and Discussion

1. Have you ever been around a conversation in your extended church family that left you confused, unsettled, or feeling divided? If so, what was your response? How could you have responded better?

2. Considering that the church is the bride of Christ, what steps can you take in the future to protect, guard, and honor the church?

3. What have you done recently that has shown support for your pastor and/or leadership?

two

Quit Giving Your Money Away

We are a baseball family. My son played baseball from age five through college. We have visited every single Major League Baseball stadium. In addition to the pictures we've taken, we have a collection of great baseball memorabilia from each stadium and from the players we've met. Now don't get upset with me, but we are Yankees fans, which is a little strange coming from a family who has lived on the West Coast their entire lives. There's a good chance you hate the Yankees—there are plenty who do. But like I always tell the haters, to date the Yankees have won twenty-seven World Series titles, so I guess they are doing something right.

My favorite games to attend have always been my son's. He is left-handed, and I love watching him pitch. I've always joked that his left arm is my retirement program. Years ago, it was a Saturday ritual to pack up some lawn chairs, put together a small ice chest, and head to the Little League field to watch our favorite player. My daughter, who is only fifteen months older than my son, had only one reason for going to the Little League field: the snack bar. Her favorite candy was Skittles, and she knew she would likely get to purchase some when she came to the field.

One Saturday we were at the Little League field cheering on our son, and in the middle of the game my daughter hit me up for some snack-bar money. I gave her enough to purchase some candy, and sure enough, she came back with a pack of Skittles. As we were watching the game, she was taking small handfuls, working through her bag of candy. I leaned over to her and said, "Can I have a few?"

I was taken aback when without hesitation she looked up at me and said, "No."

I looked at her and said, "What do you mean, no?"

She said, "I don't want to give you any."

I couldn't believe she said this to me. I was thinking, *How selfish of you. I'm your dad; can't you share? I didn't ask you for the whole bag; I just wanted a few.*

At that Little League baseball field, my daughter forgot who truly supplied those Skittles for her. Not only did she forget who her provider was—me—she wasn't even willing to give up a small portion of what she was given.

The mind-set of my daughter is often the mind-set of you and me. We forget that what we have was provided by someone else (God), and many times we are unwilling to give back a portion of what is all his to begin with. We have to quit thinking categorically that it's our money at all! It's not ours, it's his.

This may be difficult for some of us to get our mind around. We go to school, earn a degree, and work hard at a job or at a business we started, and we feel that because we did it all, we deserve it all. We are missing a crucial point here. It all belongs to God. He gave us the ability to make money. Whether we work with our hands in construction, work with numbers in an office, or use our personality skills in sales, we must remember, he gave us the ability to do the work. He is the creator of the skill and the provider of the work. He is the one who owns everything. We are simply stewards of this earth and of what he blesses us with. The Scriptures declare this over and over.

Psalm 89:11—"The heavens are Yours, the earth also is Yours; / The world and all it contains, You have founded them" (NASB).

Psalm 95:5—"The sea is His, for it was He who made it" (NASB).

Haggai 2:8—"'The silver is Mine and the gold is Mine,' declares the LORD of hosts" (NASB).

Psalm 50:10—"For every beast of the forest is Mine, / The cattle on a thousand hills" (NASB).

Deuteronomy 8:18 (my favorite)—"But you shall remember the LORD your God, for it is He who is giving you the power to make wealth" (NASB).

It's his; it's all his. Everything on the earth, in the sky, and in the sea—he owns it all. The income we make is a result of the ability he gives us to make it. We are simply stewards or managers of what he has blessed us with. When we think it's ours, we miss what Scripture clearly teaches. Our misguided mind-set keeps us from following the clear biblical principles of giving that God lays out in Scripture.

When we fall into the trap of thinking that our money is ours, when it's really his, we inadvertently follow the misplaced thinking that my daughter had. How quickly she forgot on her journey from the snack bar back to the bleachers that what she was holding in her hands was provided by someone else. When we refuse to give back to God a handful of what he has given to us, maybe he would whisper in our ears, *It's all mine; I provided it*. He owns everything and has the ability to give us more. No doubt, if he really feels it's necessary to teach us a valuable lesson, he can take it from us. Would he ever do that? Possibly. You have to always remember that God is more interested in our character than in our comfort.

God may not ask from us the entire bag of Skittles (our money); he does ask for a handful (the tithe). The Bible is clear about this. In Malachi 3 God instructs us that the tithe, which is 10 percent of our income, belongs to him. The tithe showed up in the life of Abraham (Gen. 14), which comes before the law, and it also is spoken of often after the law was given. Tithing is mentioned in both the New Testament and the Old Testament. It is God's design that we tithe, which brings support to the local church, and in return he blesses us. I have seen this over and over in my life. It is an absolutely amazing God-given promise.

But again, it's our mind-set that gets in the way. Remember that your employer is not your provider. God is your provider. If you are not careful, you will put more trust in your savings than in your Savior. When this starts to happen, you start to fall into the misguided mind-set that it all belongs to you, when in reality it all belongs to him.

We can look at history as proof that this mind-set has become common in our churches. The average attendee of a local church gives 2.5 percent of their income—way below what God has required. During the Great Depression, the average attendee gave 3.3 percent of their income.[3] During the worst economic time in our nation's history, Christians gave more to Christ and his work than we do today. One reason for the low amount of giving today is that, on average, only 10 to 25 percent of people actually follow the biblical principle of tithing.[4] So when as many as 90 percent of people don't tithe in a church, the average giving from each household drops to 2.5 percent.

> If you are not careful, you will put more trust in your savings than in your Savior.

As a pastor, it breaks my heart to see people miss out on the joy and blessing of giving. God wants so much for your life and wants to give you so much. He is looking for a partnership between you and him. One of my favorite examples of giving is the life and ministry of George Müller. He was the founder of the orphanage at Ashley Down, which housed over ten thousand children during his life. In addition, Pastor Müller established 117 schools that over 120,000 students attended, with a large portion of those students being orphans.[5] He did all of this without ever asking for funding and without ever going into debt. He was a firm believer in the Scriptures that speak of God's blessing as you walk in his will. He gave of his life, time, and resources because he followed what God said, and in return, God poured out his favor and provision. Simply put, George Müller gave, and God blessed. That's how it works.

We give, and he gives back. We let go of what's in our hands, and he lets go of what's in his. Every time the offering bucket goes by and we don't honor him through the tithe, we are leaving so much on the table. There's an abundance of God's goodness and riches that he desires to pour into our lap, and we pass it by every time we let the offering plate pass us by.

How You Win

When you give as God requires you to, you don't lose, you win. Here are just a few examples of how you win.

Giving Makes You Resemble God

God is a giver. He loves to give. It's not just something he does; it's who he is. He is a God of extreme generosity. I think of all the blessings in my life: my wife, my children, my family, the country I live in, the home I have, the finances that have been provided to me, the places I've traveled, the things I've seen, the car I drive, the freedom I experience—the list can literally go on and on. The list could go on for you as well. Sure, we've all had hard times, but we are blessed by the Creator.

Genesis 1:27 tells us that "God created human beings in his own image." The word "image" comes from the Hebrew word *tselem*, meaning something like "his drawing or his representation." Genesis is telling us that we are created in his outline. We are traced from his image. Have you ever put your hand on a piece of paper and traced your hand? The tracing is the exact shape of your hand. This is what the Scripture is teaching us. We are the exact tracing of God. We are made to imitate his character. So if he is an extravagant, generous God, then we are to be extravagantly generous as well. Giving makes us like God.

50

I've seen a lot of people who aren't Christian who are incredibly generous. What they do not realize is that they are made in God's image and are simply tracing his character. If you're a Christian, then you have to realize that you can give and not be a Christ follower, but you can't follow Christ and not give. It doesn't work. It actually doesn't make any sense. If you follow God, if you imitate his character, if you strive to be in his likeness, you have to give. It's who he is, and because he is a giver, we are to be givers as well. Remember, you are *tselem*; you are an outline of God.

> You can give and not be a Christ follower, but you can't follow Christ and not give.

Giving Is an Act of Worship

When we think of the word "worship," we typically think of singing, especially singing the slower songs, and maybe raising our hands and closing our eyes. But worship is much more than that. To worship means that we put the object of our worship above us. It's an act of obedience to God that says, "You're way above me." Worship happens when we choose to forgive when we'd rather stay angry, when we choose to love when we'd rather hate, and when we choose to give when we'd rather spend that money on other things. We obey him and follow what he says because he is first in our life. He is the voice of authority and the final word. That's what it means to worship him.

This is why giving is such an important part of our worship. It is an act of obedience. It is letting God know that he genuinely has first place in our life. Jesus said in John 14:15,

"If you love me, show it by doing what I've told you" (Message). How much clearer can Jesus make it? *If you say you love me, then do what I have asked.* Throughout Scripture, God teaches on the subject of tithing, giving, and extravagant generosity. The first established church in the book of Acts was known more for its generosity than for its theology. This is what it means to be a Christ follower—doing what he asks. Often, we want to justify our lack of obedience in the area of giving by pointing out the other areas in which we have exercised obedience, as if obedience is some sort of multiple choice. This is selective obedience, picking and choosing the areas in which we will and will not follow Christ. If he is not Lord of all, then he is not Lord at all. You can't pick and choose. Think about that in the context of a marriage. You can't say, "I will love you, but I'm not going to honor you" or "I will honor you, but I'm not going to be faithful to you." You can't pick and choose in a marriage, to follow only a portion of the vow you committed to. It doesn't work in a marriage, and it doesn't work in a relationship with Christ.

The Bible says that "Satan disguises himself as an angel of light" (2 Cor. 11:14). This means that the enemy will disguise his voice. He will make you feel like what he is saying is good and right, when the truth is that he is only pulling you away from what God wants from you and for you. We might say different things to ourselves:

God understands why I don't give.

God sees my heart.

I give through my time.

My volunteering is my tithe.

I may not tithe, but I give to those I see in need.

I've seen churches misuse money, so I'm not going to give to my church.

All of these thoughts seem logical, not like a heart of disobedience, and that's exactly what the angel of light wants you to believe. But the truth is that none of these are a reason to not tithe to the church you attend. None of them excuse you from the responsibility Jesus has placed on you to honor him with our personal finances. Again Jesus said, "If you love me, show it by doing what I've told you" (John 14:15 Message). This request of Jesus is about worship. "If you love me, then give as I have asked you to. Do what I have told you." If you struggle in this area, if reading this makes you uncomfortable, I encourage you to step out. Just do it. Start now. Begin to follow Christ through your giving, and I promise you, he will not let you down. He is ready to pour out his blessing on those who trust in him.

Giving Blesses You in Return

My wife and I live near the beach in Southern California. Over the last few years, I have taken up surfing. I say that to people, and they say, "Wow, that sounds cool." But you haven't seen me surf; it isn't that cool. I am lousy at it, but I love it. Getting out there in the water and tackling something new is a blast.

You paddle out and then sit on your board and wait for the next set of waves. If you have ever surfed, ridden a boogie board, or bodysurfed, you know exactly what I'm talking about. You wait for a set of waves to come, and you take one in. There have been countless waves over the years that I wish I would have taken but that I let go by me. You feel like you have missed out on such a good opportunity when you see the perfect wave go by. It's frustrating, because you feel like that wave was designed just for you, and for whatever reason, you let it go by.

In the same way, there are blessings that God has perfectly designed for you, a treasure that only he can provide. Each time we don't honor him by tithing, it's like missing the perfect wave—we miss out on something so good. When I'm out surfing, I know that I have to paddle; that's my job, and then there is the moment that the wave takes me, and I ride on its momentum. The financial area of our Christian life is the same way. God expects you to do your part, to tithe faithfully, and then he will do his part by fulfilling his promise. In Malachi 3:10 God says that he will open up the windows of heaven and bless your life. You paddle, he blesses. That's how it works.

How Your Church Wins

We've already learned that God wants to bless our lives. He opens the windows of heaven on those who tithe. God will bless those who obey him in their acts of generosity. That's how we win. But what about our church? How does the church—our spiritual family, our place of worship—win? To understand how our church wins, we first need to understand how it loses.

Think about it. There is so much God-given potential that the church is missing out on simply because it doesn't have the finances—not that the finances aren't in the room, because they are. There is more than enough money to do the

54

work God has called the local church to do. If every person would simply follow the God-given principles of tithing, the local church would be unleashed to accomplish more than it ever has. Imagine if everyone in your church simply started following the principle of generous giving.

How many more people could be reached?

How many more families and marriages could find hope?

How many people in need could we supply food or shelter for?

How many children could be rescued from sex trafficking?

How many more ministries could be funded to reach new and different people?

How many abused children, foster children, and handi-capped children could we bring hope and healing to?

How many more churches could we start?

How many more people would cross the line of faith and start following Jesus?

The list of all the things we could do literally goes on and on. The potential is astounding. The money is there; it's in the chairs every Sunday. God is waiting for you to be obedient. Your obedience will lead to your blessing. Your obedience will lead to any others being blessed. It is a win-win-win situation.

I remember when our church was only a couple years old. We felt like God put it in our hearts to purchase some land. This

> If every person would simply follow the God-given principles of tithing, the local church would be unleashed to accomplish more than it ever has.

55

was a big step for a church that was so young. In addition to being young itself, the church was filled with people who were young in their faith. Most of them didn't have a church background, and our church was the first church they had ever called home. The property we wanted to purchase was priced at a point that seemed impossible for such a young church. We got a small team together to run a feasibility study and came to the conclusion that we could buy it only if everyone got on board. We started to meet with key leaders, and they embraced the vision of this land. We held meetings with those who volunteered in the church, and they too embraced the vision.

I remember the day we were going to present it to the church. I was honestly nervous. I wondered how they would accept this vision-stretching project of purchasing land. To my surprise, the people responded with incredible enthusiasm. Although they were young in their faith, they truly believed that God would accomplish what seemed nearly impossible. I knew that God would come through, but I also knew that the people needed to come through. I witnessed during that season something miraculous. I saw people step up in their generosity and give like never before. I watched people, new in their faith, trust God with their finances for the first time in their lives. The stories of people who sacrificed started to roll in. I heard about people who sold their vacation home or put their extra car up for sale. One person sold their boat, and one person even sold a small plane that they had inherited years ago and gave the entire amount to our project. Unbelievable!

More people gave than I had ever seen, and the church was able to do something that we all thought was close to impossible. And of course, the stories of God blessing these people with new jobs and more business came rolling in as well. I saw with my own eyes the potential of a local church. Regardless of size or how old or young your church is, the potential is huge. God wants your church to win, but he needs those who belong to the church to step to the plate and start swinging. God has created what I call a success cycle:

- God blesses us with finances (our job, our business, etc.).
- We bless him back through our tithe and offering.
- He then uses that to change the world (and we get to be a part of it).
- He then blesses us with even more finances, and the cycle repeats.

Don't rob God, don't rob your church's potential, and don't rob yourself. He's a big God, and he wants to do big things. Do your part, and I promise he will do his.

But I Can't Afford to Give

You might be thinking right now, *I totally agree. I can see how God clearly states in Scripture what he wants us to do when it comes to the subject of tithing and giving. I can see how God is waiting to bless our lives and how the local church that I call home could do so much more for the kingdom of God if every person would give as God requires.* But even thinking this and believing this, you still think, *I can't afford it.*

Most of the time when someone tells me that they can't afford to tithe, it's because they have gotten themselves into debt. They are overextended. They have spent more than they make. Unfortunately this is a common problem in America. As a matter of fact, the *New York Times* reported that in 2008, when we went into a recession, America had accumulated an astounding consumer debt of $12.68 trillion. But after declining for nineteen straight quarters, debt started to rise again, and by 2017 household debt had reached $12.73 trillion, surpassing the debt we had going into the recession.[6] We didn't learn our lesson. Broad surveys show that Americans are living with debt:

- The average credit-card debt in America is $16,883.
- The average car loan debt in America is $29,539.
- The average student loan debt in America is $50,626.
- The average interest paid on credit cards per year is $1,292.[7]

This may be where you find yourself—in a position of debt due to school loans, credit cards, auto loans, boat loans, mortgages, or some other form of debt that has wrapped itself around you and left you feeling like you are drowning in a sea of bills and payments. Proverbs 22:7 describes it this way: "The borrower is servant to the lender."

If this is you, I strongly encourage you to fight your way out of debt. Get the counsel you need, and get on the pathway to freedom. You may have wandered into debt, but you cannot wander out; you have to have a plan. Once you start moving toward getting out of debt, you will start feeling hope. Every time you knock out another debt, you will feel more and more liberated. Realize how much this debt is costing you. In addition to the insane amount of money wasted on interest, it is robbing you of so much. It robs you of joy, creates stress, burdens your relationships, and limits what you can do for the kingdom of God. There is nothing good that comes from debt. So again, get the counsel you need, create a plan, and start fighting your way out of debt. It may not be easy, but it will be worth it.

This debt may be what is causing you to say, "I can't afford it." So the temptation is to say, "As soon as I get out of debt, I will start honoring God with my finances." I understand the thinking here, and it seems logical. However, God doesn't say the tithe belongs to him after you get out of debt, straighten out your finances, or get your affairs in order. The tithe belongs to him, period. You have to believe and trust that God is not going to fail you. Even if the math does not add up on paper, you have to trust that when God has his hand on your finances, it will add up. The first step in getting out of debt is to put God first in your finances. You need his help. When you keep your finances in your hands, you take them out of God's hand. Believe me, you don't want that.

At the root of all of this is trust. Do we trust God to meet our needs? Will he really take care of us? Proverbs 3:5 teaches us, "Trust in the LORD with all your heart; do not depend on your own understanding." That is sometimes hard to do, especially in our finances. But it's what God requires of us. If you think about it, it's the only way to truly have a relationship with God. Without trust, there can be no intimacy. You can't have genuine intimacy with anyone if you don't have trust.

When the enemy showed up in Genesis 3 to tempt Eve, what did he tempt her with? Did he tempt her with pride?

No. Did he tempt her with lust? No. Did he tempt her with greed? No. Of all the things he could have tempted Eve with, the enemy tempted her with trust. He said to her in verse 1: "Did God really say you must not eat the fruit from any of the trees in the garden?" In essence, he was saying, "Can you really trust what God says?" He knew that if he could get Eve to not trust in God, he could destroy Eve's intimacy with God. That is the goal of the enemy: to destroy our relationship with God. So the enemy goes after trust. If he can get us to not trust in God, then he can keep us from experiencing true intimacy with our Savior.

God can be trusted. He is your spiritual Dad, and your Dad is very, very, very rich. He can handle whatever financial challenges you face. Trust him. If you don't, you will rob yourself of intimacy with God, and you will be keeping his hand away from your finances, which is the last thing you want to do. Trust him. Start tithing. If you're in debt, get out. His promises are true, and he never goes back on them. You will win. Your church will win. Start today, and see what God does.

Questions for Study and Discussion

1. Considering the statement "He is either Lord of all or not at all," would you be able to say that God is Lord over all areas of your life? Explain.

2. What matters do you need to settle in your heart today regarding finances and your personal walk with God?

3. Where can you make a change in this area? Take some time to pray right now by yourself or with your group. Make a verbal commitment about a change you are going to make.

three

Quit Helping Out

Several years ago, my wife and I were invited by some people to have dinner at their house. These people were great, but in the conversations I had had with them in the past, there just wasn't a lot of chemistry. Saturday evening rolled around, and I begrudgingly got ready. I'm sure I was mumbling a few complaints as I got dressed, but my wife kindly ignored them, and soon we were on our way to their house. It actually turned out to be a pretty good evening. Great meal, good conversation, and a few laughs. I could see in my wife's eyes that she was thinking of me and wanting to say, with a loving voice, "I told you so." But in her normal patient demeanor, she refrained. I remember after dinner I helped to clear the table and clean up. I honestly didn't do a lot. They kept saying, "You don't need to do anything. Just relax. You're our guest." But I continued to help, and they were grateful. They thanked me several times. They obviously were not expecting me to do anything. I was their guest. I wasn't the host or the owner of the home. I didn't belong to the family. I was simply visiting, and because of that, they didn't expect me to help. They didn't make me feel obligated to help, but I did.

We finished up our evening, and they walked us out to our car. We thanked them for having us over and said goodbye. We drove home, and as my wife and I pulled up to our house, I noticed the trash cans were still out. So before I went into the house, I brought the trash cans in. When I went inside, my wife was washing a few dishes that were in the sink, so as we talked, I dried the dishes and put them away.

There wasn't any discussion about me bringing in the trash cans or drying the dishes. At the house we were at earlier that evening, there was a big discussion about me helping out, but not at my home. Why? Because when I am a guest at someone's house, it's different. There isn't a big expectation for me to do anything. But when I am at my house, I am part of the family and so am expected to do things, to take care of what's needed.

If you have children, you probably teach them the same thing. You have probably given them the parental speech that says, "This is our house, you are a member of this family, and as a member of this family, you are expected to do your part." When you give them this speech, you are attempting to correct their thinking. You want to shift their mind-set from thinking *Mom and Dad should do everything* to *I am a member of this family, and we all do our part.*

The guest mind-set can often find its way into the church. Maybe we don't mean to think this way, but we do. We view ourselves as guests rather than as members of God's family. Thinking this way causes us to feel that it is someone else's responsibility to serve, to volunteer, to give of their time and talent. This is not at all what Paul meant when he said, "We are all members of one body" (Eph. 4:25 NIV). This statement from the Word of God changes everything.

Think about your body. The hand, the foot, and the arm all have a purpose. Without them, your body suffers. This is also true with the body of Christ. We are all different parts, and when one part doesn't participate, the entire body suffers. When one person stands on the sideline and leaves it up to everyone else, then the church, the body of Christ, is weakened. We are better together, and we all were meant to serve together.

If we are believers and we attend a local church, we are not guests in that church. We are part of a family: God's family. Just as kids have responsibilities in their family, so we as Christians have a responsibility to serve, to give our time, and to make our talents and gifts available for the advancement of God's kingdom and of the church we attend. As seen in Scripture, this is not an option but rather an expectation of the Lord.

We see this in the story of Nehemiah when he rallied the people to rebuild the walls of Jerusalem. It took everyone doing their part. No one was excluded. Or in the book of Acts, everyone served in the first local church. Everyone did their part. From Old Testament to New, we see that God's blueprint for the local church is that it is a family, and family serves together.

At South Hills, the church in which I serve as lead pastor, we always say it this way: "We don't have members, we have owners. Membership is about rights; ownership is about responsibility." I am not saying I am for or against membership in a church. What I am saying is that I am against the mind-set that says, "I have rights but I don't have responsibilities."

We want the people of South Hills to realize that this is their church. You see, owners treat things differently. Have you ever been to a small sandwich shop or an independently owned café? In many cases you will notice a big difference between the way an employee treats you and the way the owner treats you. There's a difference between how an employee approaches the business and how the owner approaches the business. The attitude, mind-set, actions, reactions, and the overall approach are completely different. The owner sweeps when the floor is dirty, cleans up when things are messy, and strives to be sure the customers are satisfied and the business is growing. This is what God is looking for.

> Membership is about rights; ownership is about responsibility.

We know it's God's house. But remember that we are his children, and that means that we do our part. Your pastor is not meant to do it all—that is wrong thinking. The responsibility doesn't fall on the person sitting next to you, in front of you, or behind you at church. The responsibility falls on you. The church that you attend is your family, and you have a spiritual responsibility to serve in and through that family.

By Nature We Are Radically Self-Absorbed

In addition to an unhealthy and misguided mind-set that says "I am a guest" rather than "I am part of this family," the other challenge is that, by nature, we are self-absorbed. It is part of our sinful nature to think more often of ourselves than we do of others. Everything in our society screams that the most important person on the planet is you. This problem started with Adam and Eve, continued with their offspring Cain and Abel, and has continued on through each generation. Jesus had to fight to correct this wrong view even in his own disciples. Look at this conversation found in Mark 10:33–37:

> "Listen," he said, "we're going up to Jerusalem, where the Son of Man will be betrayed to the leading priests and the teachers of religious law. They will sentence him to die and hand him over to the Romans. They will mock him, spit on him, flog him with a whip, and kill him, but after three days he will rise again."
>
> Then James and John, the sons of Zebedee, came over and spoke to him. "Teacher," they said, "we want you to do us a favor."
>
> "What is your request?" he asked.
>
> They replied, "When you sit on your glorious throne, we want to sit in places of honor next to you, one on your right and the other on your left."

What a crazy, albeit humorous, story. Jesus is sharing about his death and the agony he is going to face, and the only response from James and John is to say, "We want the best seats in heaven, the ones right next to you." There is no consideration of what Jesus is going through, no thought of how they could serve this person who is facing a difficult challenge. The only response is one centered in complete and utter selfishness. Jesus had already spent countless hours with these disciples, and after all this, they still didn't get it. They had somehow failed to see that they were part of

God's family and that, as part of his family, they were called to serve. The opportunities to war against your self-absorbed human nature are in front of you every week.

Your church has places for you to serve, and Christ wants you to serve there. This may not be a normal thing where you work or maybe even with the friends you associate with. Maybe that was the problem with the disciples. They didn't grow up in church, so the idea of serving others through the body of Christ was foreign to them. People around them were very self-absorbed: religious leaders, tax collectors, and high-ranking officials were all out for themselves. Knowing this, Jesus took advantage of the moment and responded to the disciples' selfishness by saying this:

> You know that the rulers in this world lord it over their people, and officials flaunt their authority over those under them. But among you it will be different. Whoever wants to be a leader among you must be your servant, and whoever wants to be first among you must be the slave of everyone else. For even the Son of Man came not to be served but to serve others and to give his life as a ransom for many. (Mark 10:42–45)

Did you catch what Jesus says there? He points out to the disciples that many people around them flaunt their authority and do not serve others but only serve themselves. Then he says, "But among you it will be different." In essence he is saying that if you are going to be a part of his family, you are not going to be self-absorbed or expect everyone else to serve while you stand on the sidelines. If you have children, you have probably said something similar: "This is not the way we act in our family. This is not what we do. Instead, this is what we stand for." What you're letting your children know is that because they are part of the family, they have responsibilities in the family. There are expectations for being part of that family. This is what Jesus is saying to us. Other people can stand on the sideline, think only of themselves, and never serve—but among you, it will be different.

Find a Need and Fill It

Years ago, a successful businessman started attending our church. He was an entrepreneur at heart and had built a thriving business from the ground up. He started attending because the church that he had recently called home had shut its doors. We connected almost immediately. He had a contagious spirit, and I loved his enthusiasm for life and for the Lord. I did not ask anything of him over the next few months, primarily because I knew he had had a difficult experience in his former church, and I figured that he needed some time to refresh and be ministered to. After a few months, we were out to lunch, and he said to me, "I notice there is a problem at the church."

I jokingly said, "Only one?"

He laughed and replied, "Seriously. On Sunday morning it seems that there aren't really any backstage hands—people who are designated to bring the table and chair out for your preaching, move around audio equipment as needed, and generally ensure that everything behind the scenes is functioning as it should."

I told him, "Yeah, you're right. We lost the leader that was heading that up, and we have someone filling in."

He immediately responded, "I'll take care of it. How many people are helping out right now?"

I said, "Just a few."

He said, "Well, we have several services, so I figure we will need at least fifteen people on the team. Get me the names of the people who are currently helping, and I'll make it happen."

When I returned to the office, I emailed him the names and contact info.

The next Sunday, he was in full recruiting mode. I saw him approaching people to see if they would help. He had revised the former leader's job description for volunteers. Over the next thirty days, he got over fifteen people plugged in to the ministry. He had properly functioning headsets, branded T-shirts, and a team that was united and moving forward. He did an outstanding job of putting it all together, and he did it in thirty days.

After about four or five months, he approached me again. He said, "Pastor Chris, I've got this ministry humming. I have put a leader over it, and they will keep it moving forward. It no longer needs me." Then he looked at me and said, "Now what do you need me to do?"

This man was busy. He had had four children under age eighteen, owned his own company, and traveled like crazy, yet he still managed to make a difference. The other part of the story I love is that I didn't approach him; he approached me. He modeled what I believe God wants from those who attend a local church: find a need and fill it. Your church has plenty of needs: places to get involved, positions to fill, and even some ministries that need someone to revamp them, like my friend did. You don't need to wait for someone to approach you, for the pastor to preach a message that will motivate you, or for the annual ministry fair. You can start now. You can start today. Find a need and fill it.

How You Win

Here's a simple and clear truth: God created you to serve. Because he created you to serve, and because he is a loving God who desires to bless you, he has set aside some benefits that are given to you when you serve. Here are just a few of the amazing things that God has in store for those who step off the sidelines and get in the game.

Serving Provides You with Purpose and Fulfillment

There may be several things in your life that bring you purpose and fulfillment. You might have a job that you love and that gives you a sense of meaning. Maybe you have a great marriage that brings you much fulfillment. You might be a parent who finds purpose, as you should, in the great responsibility of leading your children in the right direction. All of these things are great, and I hope that you are experiencing them in your personal life. But please hear me: there is still a piece of your heart that will never experience fulfillment until you begin to use your time and talents to serve the kingdom of God. It isn't because your job, marriage, or children aren't important; it's because the Creator made you this way. There is nothing you can do to fill the portion of your heart that has been reserved for serving God.

When I was a kid, my parents bought us a game called Perfection. There were several plastic pieces in different

71

shapes: circles, squares, triangles, stars, half-moons, and lots more. There were probably twenty or more shapes. The object of the game was to place the shapes in the holes on the board. You had to get all the shapes in the right holes before the timer ran out. No matter how hard you tried— and believe me, I tried hard—you could not put one shape in another shape's hole. It wouldn't fit. You could try to cram it in there, but it would never work. Each piece would fit in one specific place, and no matter what you did, nothing else could go in its place. This is what it is like when it comes to your heart and the pieces God has put into play. You can try all you want to find fulfillment and purpose with other pieces, but they won't fit. It's not the way that God designed your heart. You were created for purpose. You were created to serve in his kingdom. There may be many great things in your life that bring you fulfillment, but you will still come up short if you don't serve with your time and talent.

First Peter 4:10 says it this way: "God has given each of you a gift from his great variety of spiritual gifts. Use them well to serve one another." Few things are clearer than this short Scripture. It is God who gives us a gift. And he provides this gift to be utilized for his kingdom, for us to serve one another. Peter was encouraging believers to use their gifts to serve each other in their churches. In the second verse of this book, he tells them, "God the Father knew you and chose you." It was true for them, and it's true for you. God has chosen you and called you. You were created to serve others through the local church. If the Lord created you this way, then nothing will ever be able to take its place. You were born to serve!

Serving Nourishes the Soul

If you have ever been in a place where you served someone in need, you know exactly what I mean when I say that serving nourishes the soul. Maybe you've had the chance to go to an impoverished country or have served the poor and needy in some way, and you walked away saying, "I think I got more out of serving them than they got out of me." There was something special about it. Something happened deep inside of your spirit. It refreshed you, inspired you, and brought a deep sense of joy and fulfillment that you may never have felt before. Think about that for a moment. You served others by giving your time, talent, and maybe even resources, and somehow you walked away feeling more blessed than they did. How is that possible? Because God created you to serve. It's in your DNA. When you respond to what he has called you to do, it brings a sense of life to your soul.

After Jesus spent time with the woman at the well, ministering to her and serving her, the disciples approached him and urged him to eat. His response was unexpected. He said, "I have a kind of food you know nothing about" (John 4:32). He went on to tell them in verse 34: "My nourishment comes from doing the will of God." Jesus was explaining that there is a kind of nourishment for our souls that can only come when we serve God, and one of the primary ways we serve God is by serving others. That's why when I have served the poor and needy or have done some work in an impoverished country, I have walked away feeling refreshed and renewed in my spirit. There is a kind of food or nourishment that is provided by God when I serve others.

73

Serving Provides Health Benefits

I won't spend a lot of time on this topic, but I think it is amazing that God created us in such a way that there are actual health benefits to serving. Serving or volunteering can bring an increase in quality of relationship, boost your self-esteem, make you happier, reduce stress, and lengthen your life expectancy.[8]

How loving is our God? We already know that he created us to serve others through the local church. He not only created us to do it, but he expects us to. It is part of being in his family. Remember what Jesus said: "But among you it will be different." So he creates us this way and places a responsibility on us to respond, but then, in his divine love, he attaches benefits to serving, benefits that have been spoken by God and proven through science. He doesn't have to do that. He could just instruct us to serve and not give us any reward for it; but he does. He is so good! When you serve, others win and you win!

> When you serve, others win and you win!

How Your Church Wins

I have bought into Bill Hybels's statement that "the local church is the hope of the world."[9] The church is the place where people in communities big or small find hope, healing, and relationships. God's master plan was that the church, including your church, would be the change agent for the world. You might attend a small church or a big church. You might be in a town where everyone knows your name, or you might be in a metropolitan area. No matter your location, God has created your church to be a lighthouse to a world in need.

With this great call comes great responsibility for those who call that church home. Unfortunately, many churches across America are filled with people who have not yet followed Christ in the area of serving. As a result, the church suffers. So many ministry ideas never get off the ground and so many areas of ministry never reach their potential simply because people choose to ignore God's clear call on them to serve. Your church likely has several areas in which you could serve: children's, youth, worship, tech, greeters, ushers, hospitality, creative arts, office help, and many more. Of course, this doesn't include the ministry possibilities that haven't yet begun because there isn't the manpower or womanpower to pull it off. There are plenty of opportunities to serve in the church you attend. All you need to do is say yes. When you do, your church wins. Your church begins to reach its potential because you removed yourself from the sidelines and got in the game. More people serving means greater results and greater impact for your church.

Years ago, after one of our morning services, I met a couple in their late thirties who attended South Hills. They approached me and shared that they had started coming to the church about eighteen months prior but still hadn't gotten involved. They said they realized that God calls each of us to serve, and they can't sit in the chairs each week thinking that someone else will do it. They have to do their part because they are part of the family—something they had obviously heard before in one of our weekend services. They went on to say that they loved children and knew there was always a need for more volunteers in that area, so they wanted to get

75

involved. I connected them to the appropriate leaders, and, after the standard vetting process, they were serving.

After a few months had gone by, I saw them in between services and thought I would ask them how it was going. They were so excited. They said, "Pastor, we absolutely love serving in the children's department. We love investing in the future generation, and we finally feel like we are in the game." I told them how proud I was of them for taking ownership in the church and for not having the mind-set that it was someone else's responsibility. They went on to tell me, "Pastor, we have an idea. We live in a small apartment building, and there are lots of children around. In the middle of the apartment complex is a small playground area with picnic benches. We were thinking of running an after-school Bible study for kids in the playground area. We could do some crafts, teach a lesson, and maybe as a result some of these kids and their parents will find Christ. What do you think?"

Of course, like any pastor, I was totally pumped. I said, "Yes, I love it! I absolutely think you should do it." So with big, servant hearts they went after it. Over the next few months they told me how many kids were coming to their Bible studies and all the great things that were happening. As time progressed, they started showing up to church with some of the kids and their parents from their after-school Bible study. It was seriously amazing and undoubtedly pleased the heart of God.

I love the heart of this couple. They found a need and filled it. They got involved, and as a result, they won and the church won. They won because they were following God's clear calling and their hearts were filled with a sense of greater purpose. The church won because more children were served on Sunday and more people were reached through the apartment Bible study—and as a result the church grew. That is what I call a win-win situation.

Don't wait for tomorrow to get involved. Start today. Find a place in your church to serve, and go all in. God has called you to serve. You were created for it. Don't think that it's someone else's responsibility, not yours, to serve. That isn't true. Remember what Jesus said: "But among you it will be different." If we are part of his family, then we have to serve; it's part of the deal. As we serve, God rewards us with a **Find a place in your** sense of purpose. He nourishes our soul **church to serve,** and showers multiple blessings on our life. **and go all in.** And of course our church wins. It reaches more people, serves more people, and has greater impact. So what are you waiting for? Get off the sidelines and get in the game. Your Coach is calling you by name!

Questions for Study and Discussion

1. Are there times when you stand on the sidelines and wait for others to serve? Why do you think you do that?

2. Is there a service opportunity you know God is nudging you toward? Explain.

3. What was your best serving experience? How did it impact others? How did it make you feel? How did it affect your life?

4. Where could you start serving this week? Where do you see a need? Don't pigeonhole yourself into serving in one specific area. We are all uniquely gifted. One way to discover or rediscover the areas where you will thrive is to *serve* your way to discovery. Find a place to start serving, and commit to begin this week. Everyone wins!

four

Quit Hoping People Will Come

In June 2014, I received a call from my older sister. Our mom had been a little sick lately and had gone to the doctor to see if they could figure out what was wrong. They had run a few tests and had arrived at a diagnosis: cancer. It had spread throughout her entire body. My sister called me to break the news, and needless to say, I was devastated. She said the doctors were giving Mom only ninety days to live. I couldn't believe it: unless God chose to do an absolute miracle, Mom was going to pass away in the next ninety days.

Mom made the decision to spend her days at home rather than in a hospital. Over the next several weeks, I visited her as often as I could. She faced her difficulty with such courage, strength, and assurance that it could only have come from Jesus. She managed every day with a beautiful sense of grace. She had set aside certain gifts for her children and grandchildren—not gifts that she purchased from a store, but small items she had cherished through the years that she wanted to pass down to the next generation. She didn't wait until she passed for us to receive these gifts; she gave them to us one by one.

One of Mom's favorite holidays was Christmas. She would go all out during the holiday season. Because she loved it so much, we decided that we would have a very special Christmas day in July. We got a tree and decorated it, bought her grandchildren presents (which they loved), cooked a traditional Christmas meal, and, on a very hot July day, we had Mom's final Christmas. It was a great day. We ate, laughed, and enjoyed each other's company. I will never forget sitting at the table, laughing with Mom. She was laughing so hard that she said her stomach was starting to hurt. I loved that day.

A few weeks went by, and the cancer was getting aggressive. Her body deteriorated quicker than anything I had ever seen. I was on the East Coast speaking at a conference when my sister called me. She said that she was not sure how much longer Mom would make it. The nurse had stopped by to say Mom would most likely pass in the next week or so. I canceled my engagements and hopped on a plane back to California. My siblings and I spent every day and night at my parents' house. We wanted to be there with Mom for every remaining moment she had on this earth, and also to care for her in the same way she lovingly cared for us all those years.

Mom was very quiet but also could be very funny. The nurse had stopped by and told us that, based on what she saw, Mom would most likely pass in the next day or two. Later that night, we were sitting around Mom's bed, and she was having great difficulty breathing. At one point she exhaled, and there was a long pause. We thought she had passed, and we started to cry and hug each other. Then Mom, in her normal quiet humor, opened up her eyes and said, "Oops, still here." We all laughed out loud. It was just like her—trying to figure out how to bring joy to everyone else while forgetting about herself. That's just the way she was.

Two more days went by, and then on August 16, 2014, Mom passed away. I remember the last moments I spent with her. She was very weak and was in and out of consciousness, but at one moment she waved her hand toward me. I sat by her side, she put her arm around me, and I leaned down to hug her. She whispered in my ears her final words to me. She said, "Son, keep marching forward. You have more to do. I'll be watching." I will never forget these words. They have been ringing in my ears ever since. She could have said anything to me at that moment, but this is what she chose to say. These were the words that mattered most to her.

What if you were on your deathbed, with your loved ones around you? What would be your final words to them? You are not going to say something at random or say something that has very little meaning. In that last moment, with those final words, you are going to say what matters most. That's what is so powerful about someone's final words. They show what matters most to them. The words display, above all else, what they want to communicate to the people they love.

Jesus himself had this kind of moment with his disciples. His final words came after he had died, risen from the dead, and went back to meet with his disciples before leaving this earth and ascending to heaven. At this moment, he could have said anything to his disciples. He could have talked about love, kindness, holiness, obedience, compassion—there are literally hundreds of things he could have talked about. So what did he say? What were his words? What was the thing that mattered most to him? The words are found in Matthew 28:19–20: "Go and make disciples of all the nations, baptizing them in the name of the Father and the Son and the Holy Spirit. Teach these new disciples to obey all the commands I have given you. And be sure of this: I am with you always, even to the end of the age." Of all the things that Jesus could have said as his final words to the disciples, this is what he chose. These words have become known as the Great Commission. Essentially, Jesus was telling the disciples, "Reach people, and disciple them."

Most churches in America today do a fairly good job with the back half of the Great Commission: "disciple them." Some churches go verse by verse through the Bible. Some pride themselves on passionate worship. Some have small groups, discipleship classes, Bible studies, prayer nights, Daniel fasts, and a host of other means by which they move people toward a stronger relationship with the Lord. This is all good; there is nothing wrong with it. We should want people to move forward in their relationship with the Lord, and we should strive to make pathways for them to do so. But I challenge you with this thought: Is it possible that we have done a pretty good job with the back half of the Great Commission but not so great a job with the first part?

God Has a Brilliant Strategy to Reach Your City

Hope is a wonderful emotion but a lousy strategy. We can't simply hope people will show up to church, hope they'll find Christ, or hope their life will be forever changed by his amazing grace. We can't simply pray people will come to Christ; that's an important part of the process, but that can't be the only thing we do. Some people might think that it's the church's responsibility to reach people, but that makes no sense, because, remember, *you* are the church. Those are all the wrong mind-sets. The right mind-set comes down to this: God has a brilliant strategy to reach your city, *and you are it.* The strategy isn't a program or a church building, and it sure isn't your pastor's sole responsibility. Jesus cares about the people in your circle of influence, and he is looking for you to reach them. His brilliant strategy is a partnership with you and me.

Maybe it's time we stop and ask ourselves, "When was the last time I brought someone to church?" This Sunday when you go to church, look around: How many people are there because of your efforts to reach them? How many friends, coworkers, or neighbors are actively involved in your church because of the time you spent praying for them, loving them, and pointing them toward Jesus?

> God has a brilliant strategy to reach your city, *and you are it.*

The final charge of Jesus was for you and me to reach people: to connect with friends, family, coworkers, neighbors, people at the gym or the grocery store, and other people God has brought into our lives, and lovingly point them toward a relationship with our Savior. Statistically, less than 5 percent of people in America have brought someone to church and connected them to Jesus in the last twelve months.[10]

Ouch.

Years ago, I was teaching at one of the South Hills campuses. A woman in her late twenties named Stephanie had given her life to Christ during one of the morning services.

83

Afterward, I had the opportunity to talk with her. She was brand new to the faith and didn't really know what her next steps were. Over the next couple months, she started serving at one of the doors as a greeter, got baptized, and really started to grow in her new walk with God.

One day I was teaching about God's brilliant strategy to reach our city, and Stephanie took it to heart. She began to bring people to church. One Sunday, a few minutes before the service began, she walked in with a friend about her age, and they found a seat. I went over to say hello and meet her friend. This friend of hers didn't have any church background and was kind of nervous. I got to know her a little bit and assured her that she was in the right place, and a few minutes later, the service began.

After the service, I was standing near the stage talking with someone, and I noticed that Stephanie, who had been a Christian an entire sixty days, was praying with the friend she had brought to church. After they got done praying, they walked over to me. Stephanie said, "Pastor Chris, do you remember my friend that you met before the service?"

I said, "Yes, of course."

She quickly said, "I just led her to the Lord."

Before I could congratulate her friend for receiving Christ, Stephanie jumped in and said, "Yeah, I hope I did it right." The look on her friend's face was priceless. It's like she was saying, "I hope so; there's a lot riding on this." It was one of my most special moments as a pastor: watching Stephanie, a brand-new Christian, bringing her friend to church, not sure exactly what she was doing but realizing that she was part of God's brilliant strategy and had to do her part. I absolutely loved it.

Stephanie got it. She understood that she had a responsibility as part of God's family. She didn't have the misguided mind-set that makes excuses. She didn't try to say that it was someone else's responsibility or use the reasoning that she was an introvert, as though that excused her from Jesus's Great Commission. She shared her faith and invited people to church, and as a result, people found Christ.

A disciple named Matthew also caught this vision. He was brand new to a relationship with Jesus, but he knew he had to do his part in reaching people. Take a look at what Matthew did.

> As Jesus was walking along, he saw a man named Matthew sitting at his tax collector's booth. "Follow me and be my disciple," Jesus said to him. So Matthew got up and followed him.
>
> Later, Matthew invited Jesus and his disciples to his home as dinner guests, along with many tax collectors and other disreputable sinners. But when the Pharisees saw this, they asked his disciples, "Why does your teacher eat with such scum?"
>
> When Jesus heard this, he said, "Healthy people don't need a doctor—sick people do." (Matt. 9:9–12)

Did you catch what happened here? The Bible says that Matthew made a decision to follow Christ, and then sometime later he had the dinner party. We are not sure how much time "later" means, but it couldn't have been that long. So Matthew has been a Christ follower for a very short amount of time when he decides to throw a dinner party—but not just any dinner party. He invites Jesus and the disciples *and* invites several of his coworkers and friends who are far from

God. What is Matthew doing here? He is, in a very practical
and creative way, giving his friends and coworkers a chance to
meet Jesus. I can only imagine what Matthew was thinking.
*I'm not that outgoing, I don't know how to preach, I'm brand
new at this Jesus-follower thing, so what can I do? Aha! I am*
great *at throwing parties. I'll invite my new friends—Jesus
and the disciples—and my other friends, and maybe some of
my buddies will meet Christ for the first time.* He does this
as a brand-new believer, and he does it with a three-pronged
approach: *invest, invite,* and *include.*

Invest

Matthew's first thought about who he is to reach are those
who are already in his circle of influence. He doesn't start
with strangers, he doesn't go door-to-door, and he doesn't
stand on a soapbox and tell people to repent. He starts with
those he already has a relationship with. These are people
he has already been investing in through his work; some
probably lived in his neighborhood. He does this because he
has what I call "relational equity" with these people. He has
some level of trust with these people. He has shared meals,
conducted business transactions, socialized, and done who
knows what else with them. Simply put, he has established
relationships that cause them to be quick to say yes when he
invites them over for dinner.

You also have people who God has put into your circle of
influence, people who have come into some sort of relationship with you. On some level, they know you and trust you.
These people are in your circle because God put them there. It
is part of his brilliant strategy to reach the city. These people

probably aren't in my circle nor your pastor's circle—they are in your circle. God has them there and is looking for you to reach them. He is looking for you to not wait on others but to take action. Eternity is at stake!

Maybe you've been a Christian for quite some time and you have found yourself somewhat isolated from nonbelievers. Maybe this happened unintentionally, or maybe you planned it that way. In either case, it is not God's strategy for you to be isolated from people who are far from Jesus. Yes, the Bible says in Romans 12:2 to not be part of this world, but that has more to do with behavior and character. It wasn't meant to tell us that we are to be separated from those in need of Jesus. In fact, Jesus continually spent time with those far from faith. He modeled for us how to be among those who are not walking with him and to let our light shine.

I want to encourage you to invest in those far from Jesus. Spend time with them and allow those relationships to help you point them toward Christ. Do what Matthew did: have them over for dinner. Next time you get an extra ticket to the ball game, bring them along. Have a neighborhood "get to know you" barbeque, and invite people in your area to eat, hang out, and connect with each other. My wife and I have done this several times in the neighborhoods we've lived in, not because we are pastors but because we are Christians. My point is to get strategic about spending time investing in people, including those you work with, those at the gym or the grocery store, and those neighbors across the street that up to this point you've only given a casual wave to. Invest in those in your circle, and if there are a few standing slightly outside the circle, reach out, spend time with them, and bring them in. God has them there for a reason.

Invite

The second thing Matthew does is take the time to invite his friends and coworkers to a place where they could meet Jesus. You might be thinking, *Well duh, that's obvious*. But hear me out. This step is the one where we fail the most as believers. Like Matthew, some of us have lots of nonbelieving friends that we either work with or live in the same neighborhood with. Having these relationships isn't the problem. The real challenge lies in this second part, the one that Matthew seemed to do so easily: actually crossing the line in a conversation and inviting them to a place where they can meet Jesus (in your case, the church you attend).

I remember standing in the lobby at church one day. I engaged in a conversation with a middle-aged man who was visiting the church for the first time. As we were getting to know one another, he stopped me, pointed to the stage, and said, "Is that Geoff?"

He was referring to an instrumentalist who was on stage getting ready for the service to start.

I said, "Yes, that's his name."

He squinted his eyes a little bit to make sure he was seeing the right person: "He's an insurance adjuster, right?"

I said, "Yep, that's right."

Before I could ask him how he knew Geoff, he quickly said, "I'm an adjuster at the same company Geoff works at. We see each other every day. I had no idea he went to church. He never mentioned it."

I was intrigued, so I dug a little deeper and asked, "How long have you known him?"

He said, "For at least six or seven years."

Then I said, "In all those years, he never mentioned church?"

He said, "No, not at all. We've talked about a lot of things, but he never mentioned that."

Geoff was very involved in our church. He played in the band, served wherever needed, was faithful in his giving, and practiced the spiritual disciplines of prayer and reading God's Word. But in all those years of knowing this colleague, he never once had a spiritual conversation with him. He never once invited him to church. He never once gave him one of the countless invite cards we have at church for people to invite friends and family. I don't for a moment think that Geoff didn't love Jesus, and I was very grateful for the servant's heart he had. But somehow Geoff had missed that first part of Jesus's final words. If we're honest, I think we would all admit that there's a friend in our lives who knows us pretty well but does not know the most important thing about us: that we have a relationship with Jesus.

I am not saying you need to preach to your neighbors or tell them to turn or burn. That is not what Matthew did. What God calls you and me to do is simply *invest* in those who are in our circle and *invite* them. Sometimes you might have a deeper spiritual conversation—don't be afraid to go there. But often it might be a simple invitation to join you at church one Sunday. Love them enough to share what you know will change their life. Invite them to join you at the church you call home, and see what God does.

Include

Once you *invest* and *invite*, the next step is to *include* them. If they start to show an interest in your church or take any spiritual steps, include them in your church community. Get them around some of your friends at church. If you

89

serve, get them involved too. The truth is that people don't
want to just believe, they want to belong. They want to be a
part of a community. They are not looking
for friendly churches; they are looking for
friends. When I gave my life to Christ in
a local youth group, I really didn't know
what it meant. I grew in my faith, but it
took time. Honestly, it was the community
that I was invited into that kept me around.
I started making friends, going places with
them, and serving with them, and that is what made the
difference. That is what kept me around long enough to
discover a genuine relationship with Jesus Christ.

> Love them enough
> to share what
> you know will
> change their life.

Let's go back to Matthew for a moment. He was one of
Jesus's twelve disciples. He was also a tax collector, who
in those days were not popular people. After the day of
Pentecost in Acts 2, we don't hear much about Matthew.
So maybe he didn't have the charisma of some of the other
disciples. Maybe he wasn't naturally gifted to preach like
Peter. But maybe, after meeting Jesus, he sat at his house
and thought to himself, *I am not that outgoing. I am not
gifted to speak. I can't sing. But I can put on a dinner. I
can invite my friends to be at the same place Jesus will be.
I can make a difference that way.* Whatever was going on
in Matthew's heart, one thing is for sure, he didn't make
excuses. He didn't say "I'm not that gifted" or "I'm not a
natural extrovert." He did what he could do to make Jesus
known to the people in his circle. That's what we have to
do. Regardless of whether we are introverts or extroverts,
we have to make Jesus known. We have to *invest, invite,* and
include.

How You Win

You win because you get to be a part of something that has eternal significance. You win because when you begin to take action and start helping people find Jesus, you are partnering with our Savior to change lives. There is nothing more exciting than helping someone who is far away from God discover the joy of knowing him. As a matter of fact, helping people find Jesus is one of the greatest ways to keep your relationship with him alive and thriving.

My wife and I live close to Disneyland. We have been there countless times. For us, it is not as exciting as it used to be. But I remember when our kids were very small and we took them there for the first time. They were so excited to meet Mickey and Donald, to ride all the children's rides, and to get their first set of Mickey Mouse ears. That was one of the best trips my wife and I have ever had at Disneyland. Why? Because we saw Disneyland through the eyes of someone who had never seen it before. If you want to keep your relationship with Jesus exciting and new, see it through the eyes of someone who has never seen it before. When you come alongside someone and help them discover Jesus, you will win on so many levels.

How Your Church Wins

The body of Christ is the church, and that body was meant to grow and become bigger and stronger. It was meant to reach the people in its community. You are part of that body and have a role in making those things happen. When each person in the body (your church) begins to *invest*, *invite*, and

91

include, the entire church begins to win. The church begins to thrive and grow with new life. More people get involved, more leaders are raised up, more resources are brought in, and more things begin to happen. Nothing brings more life to a body than new blood. For the body of Christ, that new blood is new believers. You will see your church begin to thrive with new passion when people who have never experienced Jesus experience him for the first time.

Remember what I said at the beginning of this chapter? God has a brilliant strategy to reach your city, and you are it. The knowledge of this strategy comes with a sense of big spiritual responsibility. But what is even more sobering is that God doesn't have a plan B. We are it. We are the ambassadors of his message of grace. We are the ones who are called to deliver the hope of the gospel. I have experienced this in my own life, but have also felt the pain of not fulfilling my part of his brilliant strategy.

In the summer of 1989, I was attending Bible college and serving as the junior high pastor at Capital Christian Center in Sacramento, California. I had signed up at a gym so that I could work out in the morning before classes. When I say gym, you have to understand something. It was an extremely small gym above a racquetball club. It felt like a hotel gym, maybe a little bigger, but not much. I was broke, and it was cheap, so it worked.

There were never more than four or five people working out in this small gym, so I began to recognize the same few faces. One early morning while I was working out, in walked Ricky Berry. He was the star rookie for the Sacramento Kings NBA basketball team. He was a big deal in that city, and on this early Monday morning, he walked into my gym. I nodded at him as he walked by, but that was the extent of our interaction. I'm sure he was at that gym because it was so small and not mainstream at all. Over the next few weeks, I saw him four or five more times.

Then one morning when I was there all by myself, Ricky Berry walked in. It was only the two of us in the gym. It was a little strange being in a very small venue with such a big celebrity. I still had not said much to him. A few nods of the head and maybe a quick "Hey, what's up?" but that was about it. As I continued my workout, I felt like God clearly spoke to me and said, *I want you to talk to him about me.* I argued with God, thinking, *It's Ricky Berry. He's a celebrity. This might be awkward.* Fifteen minutes or so went by, and I felt like God said it again: *I want you to talk to him about me.* I again shrugged it off. I am very outgoing and normally don't have a problem approaching people, but I was a little starstruck. I finished my workout, grabbed my things, took a drink of water from the water fountain, headed out the door, and heard God say, *This is the last time I'm going to tell you. Go and talk to him about me.* Once again, I said no to God, but I promised that the next time I saw Ricky I would say something. I sat in my car feeling so down about what had just happened. I committed once again to never saying no when God spoke to me.

After my classes and my time at the office, I went home. It was late afternoon, and I turned the TV on. The news was reporting a special story that just broke: Ricky Berry of the Sacramento Kings had been found dead in his home. They went on to report that he had committed suicide. They found him just a couple hours after I saw him in the gym. Just a couple hours after God said to me, "This is the last

time I'm going to tell you. Go and talk to him about me."
August 14, 1989, is a day I will forever remember. It was the
day I realized that I was part of God's brilliant strategy and
that he doesn't have a plan B. With tears in my eyes, I committed to Jesus that I would never say no to his voice again
and that I would do my part in his master plan of bringing
people to the saving grace of Jesus Christ.

Please hear me. You don't ever want to have this happen
to you. Listen to his voice and follow his command. Become
an expert at *investing, inviting,* and *including.* Help people
find Jesus. Partner with your church in reaching the people in
your city. It is all part of God's brilliant strategy, and the crazy
thing is that he allows us the privilege to be a part of it all.

Questions for Study and Discussion

1. What has your concept of evangelism been? How have you seen it done or experienced it?

2. Have you been like Matthew in your realm of influence? If so, share how.

3. Maybe the concepts of *invest* and *invite* are new to you. How could you see yourself implementing this strategy in your life in the near future?

4. Who can you start with in your circle of influence? Make a list of people you can begin to invest in and ultimately invite to church, and then start reaching out to them.

five

Quit Stopping By

A few years back I went on a trip to Niagara Falls. My dad had never been there, and it was someplace he had always wanted to visit. So my son and my dad and I set off on a special trip together. I was excited to spend time with both of them, and we had a blast. One of the tours we went on was a walking tour that takes you very close to the falls. They warned us that we would get wet and that we needed to put on the plastic ponchos they provided. Sure enough, we got drenched. After finishing the tour, I pulled out my cell phone, and it was soaked. It was still on, but it wasn't functioning properly. I couldn't text, email, go online, or make a call. It was incredibly frustrating. It's like your whole world stops when your cell phone isn't working.

You've been there before. You know how frustrating it can be. Something you have relied on, something that has been dependable day in and day out, suddenly isn't dependable

97

anymore. If you're like me, you probably didn't really appreciate its dependability until it was gone.

Noticing Dependability

There are a lot of qualities that we admire in people—kindness, courage, patience, perseverance, success, brilliance, knowledge, generosity, and many others. Dependability rarely makes the list. You don't hear about it very often. You don't see it on motivational posters. It's just not something that is often recognized. But it should be.

Here's the key: you don't notice dependability when it's there, but you sure notice it when it's not. I don't think about all the things my cell phone does every day: the texts it sends out across thousands of miles, the emails it receives almost instantaneously, the connections it makes to other states and countries around the world. I never think about my cell phone's dependability—or at least I didn't until it got soaked. And I am sure you are the same way. There are a lot of things that we depend on but never notice until they are not dependable; we expect our cars to start, our showers to be hot, and our electricity to stay on.

God is different. He sees the qualities that matter. He sees the characteristics that go unnoticed by many of us. Dependability lives in the heart of God. The Bible describes his faithfulness over and over. One of my favorite verses on God's dependability is Deuteronomy 7:9: "Know this: GOD, your God, is God indeed, a God you can depend upon. He keeps his covenant of loyal love with those who love him and observe his commands for a thousand generations" (Message). God's dependability is not just something he does;

it's who he is. It's who he wants us to be. God takes note of those who are dependable, and he rewards those who are faithful. Scripture is clear about this. Stories of people like Job and parables like the one Jesus shared regarding the talents shout of God's desire for us to show dependability and faithfulness. It displays what God is looking for and what he rewards and blesses.

But so often when it comes to Sunday morning or other church events, we just can't seem to make it on a regular basis. We may stop by, or we may not. Something might come up. Maybe part of us hopes something does.

Years ago, attending church on Sunday morning simply wasn't optional. Businesses shut down and sports leagues did not operate on Sunday morning. Sunday was a day to be in church. It was a day that you were with your spiritual family. But that has changed. The commitment to being in church each week has waned. We are not as faithful to our spiritual families as we used to be. I think we could argue that society has changed, and I would agree with that, but God hasn't. He never changes. He doesn't want us to approach the church that we call home with such a casual commitment. I like the way I once heard Joel Osteen put it: "You can be committed to church and not committed to Christ. But you cannot be committed to Christ and not be committed to the church." If we are committed to Christ, then we have to be committed to our spiritual family. You can't separate the two.

> God takes note of those who are dependable, and he rewards those who are faithful.

Author and speaker Thom Rainer wrote an article he titled "The Number One Reason for the Decline in Church

Attendance and Five Ways to Address It." In this article, he talked about how statistics show a decline in church attendance nationwide, but there is a primary reason that is overlooked for why this is happening:

> The number one reason for the decline in church attendance is that members attend with less frequency than they did just a few years ago. Allow me to explain.
>
> If the frequency of attendance changes, then attendance will respond accordingly. For example, if 200 members attend every week, the average attendance is, obviously, 200. But, if one-half of those members miss only one out of four weeks, the attendance drops to 175.
>
> Did you catch that? No members left the church. Everyone is still relatively active in the church. But attendance declined over 12 percent because half the members changed their attendance behavior slightly.[11]

The problem is that many people approach church attendance with less and less commitment. When Sunday morning rolls around, if there is a perceived better option than attending church, many people take it. And this puts a lot of pressure on pastors. If your pastors are like many other pastors, they probably deal with the pressure of building a church and creating momentum. Your pastors love the city and want to reach it. They want to create a church that is thriving and growing and that feels alive when people visit. However, they are continually competing

"You can be committed to church and not committed to Christ. But you cannot be committed to Christ and not be committed to the church."

with so many other challenges: summertime weather, sunshine, a game on TV, a special event in town, kids' sporting events, the call of the river or the beach or the mountains. We as pastors want it to be warm enough for you to come to church but not so warm that you go somewhere else and not so cold that you stay home. Funny as this sounds, it is true.

I totally understand getting away. I believe that God wants us to rest, get away, spend time with the family. But the frequency of church attendance is changing, and it's not changing for the good. Our commitment to the body of Christ is lessening, and it's not what God intended for his family. He desires for us to be committed to him and to the spiritual family that we call the local church. He is looking for us to be the type of people who are dependable in this commitment. God rewards and honors our dependability with our worship times together. It may go unnoticed by others, but it *never* goes unnoticed by God.

After four hundred years of slavery, Moses, under the guidance of the Lord, led the people of Israel to freedom. The Israelites were moving toward a promised land that God had said would be theirs. During their travels, they had come up against an enemy called Amalek. It was at this time that Moses was led to climb a mountain and pray. Look at what happened:

> While the people of Israel were still at Rephidim, the warriors of Amalek attacked them. Moses commanded Joshua, "Choose some men to go out and fight the army of Amalek for us. Tomorrow, I will stand at the top of the hill, holding the staff of God in my hand."

So Joshua did what Moses had commanded and fought the army of Amalek. Meanwhile, Moses, Aaron, and Hur climbed to the top of a nearby hill. As long as Moses held up the staff in his hand, the Israelites had the advantage. But whenever he dropped his hand, the Amalekites gained the advantage. (Exod. 17:8–11)

It isn't Moses that I want to focus on; it's his two sidekicks, Aaron and Hur. They climbed a mountain with their leader, or pastor if you will. They had no idea how long they would be on the mountain, no idea what they were going to do on the mountain, no idea what would happen when they got there. They were simply being the type of men that could be counted on. They were being dependable. Moses was the spiritual leader. The children of Israel were the spiritual family, sort of like the local church you call home. Aaron and Hur were expressing and modeling dependability to their pastor and their church (I'm taking a little liberty on the words "pastor" and "church," but I think you get what I am saying).

Predetermined Dependability

Aaron and Hur had what I call "predetermined dependability." What does that mean? It simply means that they predetermined, before they knew what the conditions would be, that they would be dependable. This is a choice you make before you know what else might happen. Now let's translate that to our commitment to the body of Christ, and particularly to our Sunday morning worship. Decide in advance that for you and your family, attending church is a nonnegotiable, that it is a priority regardless of how great the weather is, what game is on TV, or what other event comes your way. You decide beforehand that when the weekend rolls around, you go to church. Yes, you will do lots of other fun things, but they will not take the place of you and your family being in church. You are dependable; you don't skip out. You are committed to Christ, and that commitment includes being someone your spiritual family can depend on.

You might feel like your dependability at church doesn't make a big difference, but it does. It makes a difference in your marriage. Keeping Christ at the center of your marriage is an important step in having a healthy relationship, and part of that is being in church together, worshiping together, honoring Jesus together. It makes a difference in your children. You need to know that your kids are watching to see if you are going to be faithful to honor God on the Sabbath or not. If they see your dependability as a loose or casual commitment, don't be surprised if they approach Christ in the same manner when they grow up. It makes a difference in your church. It's your faithfulness that challenges fellow church members. It may be some words you share in the hallway that changes them. It may be seeing you week after week that shapes their own spiritual journey. Who knows what it will be? You are a part of the body of Christ, and that body needs you, and so does your marriage and your children. Somebody somewhere is depending on your dependability.

Let's go back for a moment to the story of Moses and his sidekicks, Aaron and Hur. There they are on top of the mountain. The battle is happening below them. As long as

Moses holds his staff high in the air, the people of Israel have the advantage, but as soon as his arms drop, they begin to lose the fight. Let's pick up the story at verse 12: "Moses' arms soon became so tired he could no longer hold them up. So Aaron and Hur found a stone for him to sit on. Then they stood on each side of Moses, holding up his hands. So his hands held steady until sunset." Look at what happened here. Moses's arms start to get tired. So Aaron and Hur find a rock for him to sit on, and then they stand on both sides of Moses, holding his arms up. Aaron and Hur up to this point had no idea what they were doing on the mountain. They were simply expressing faithfulness to God and being dependable to their leader and spiritual family. But God needed them on that mountain. Moses, their leader, needed them on that mountain. And so did their spiritual family, fighting below. People were depending on their dependability.

It would have been so easy for Aaron and Hur to say, "It's hot, I don't want to climb the mountain," to find an excuse for why they didn't want to go. But they chose what was right over what was easy. When it comes to our home church, we can find all sorts of reasons to skip Sunday services: We are a little under the weather. We've got a birthday party to attend. The kids have Little League. The kids have soccer practice. We haven't spent time together as a family lately. One of the kids has a sore throat. It's been a long week and we need to sleep in. And the list goes on and on.

Sometimes they're somewhat lame excuses, and sometimes they are legitimate. It's during these times that we have to choose what is right over what is easy. Again, I realize there are vacations and other reasons why this happens, and I am not saying these are wrong or that missing a Sunday is the end of the world, because it's not. But statistically, the number of times people attend church during the average month is dropping, and so it is going in the opposite direction of what God wants. It affects the local church, it affects our spiritual journey, it affects our spiritual families, and it affects our marriages and children.

> Spiritual maturity is choosing what is right over what is easy.

Spiritual maturity is choosing what is right over what is easy, and I strongly believe this includes our dependability at the local church level.

How You Win

This idea of being dependable to your home church is something that God speaks to throughout Scripture. Hebrews 10:25 says, "And let us not neglect our meeting together, as some people do, but encourage one another, especially now that the day of his return is drawing near." Jesus himself modeled it so much that it was recognized by Luke, who noted, "And as His *custom* was, [Jesus] went into the synagogue on the Sabbath day" (Luke 4:16 NKJV, emphasis added). The custom, habit, and dependability of Jesus himself being gathered for worship with God's people was so consistent that instead of simply saying, "He went into the synagogue," Luke points out that it was his "custom." Jesus modeled the importance of making gathering with God's people a regular habit in our lives. Jesus needed to be with other God followers each week to worship. He didn't miss it—it was his custom. So if Jesus needed it, I would think we need it

105

to. When we follow the example of Jesus in this area, and we follow God's Word on this subject, we receive rewards and blessings in our personal life.

You Set Your Children Up for Success

In Numbers 14, God speaks about a hero in the Bible, Caleb, the man who believed and trusted God for the impossible. He said that Caleb was loyal and that he could be counted on. He spoke of Caleb being dependable. Earlier we spoke of Aaron and Hur and how dependable they were to God and to their spiritual family. Here's something you may not know: Hur was the son of Caleb. Caleb as a father modeled to his family faithfulness and dependability. So no wonder his son Hur was faithful as well; he had seen it in his dad. He was simply doing what he saw his dad do all those years.

> If you want your children to walk with Jesus, then you walk with Jesus.

I often say that kids don't do what you say, they do what you do. If you want your children to walk with Jesus, then you walk with Jesus. If you want them to have a Christlike marriage, then you have a Christlike marriage. If you want your children to be plugged in to a spiritual family, to be involved in a local church, then you have to do that. It's not a guarantee that your children will be part of a church when they become adults, but if you model faithfulness in your faith, you drastically increase the odds that your children will have a strong faith when they become adults.[12] Be the example your children need by being dependable to the house of God.

God Rewards Dependability

You don't have to look any further than the story of Job to know how God responds to faithfulness and dependability. Job went through some of the toughest challenges an individual can face: rejection, financial hardship, physical setbacks. And yet in all of it Job was faithful. At the end of the story, God responded to Job being faithful by restoring his health and doubling his wealth. God sees when we are dependable to the areas that he requests of us, and when we are consistent and do what he says, he rewards it.

There are not only spiritual benefits that God showers on us when we exercise dependability to his house; there are practical ones as well. Studies show the beneficial effects of church attendance. Here are just a few:

Longer life expectancy—A 2016 study conducted by the Harvard T. H. Chan School of Public Health found that attending religious services weekly led to a significant decrease in risk of premature death.[13]

Higher quality of living—Dr. Patrick Fagan found that when at-risk youth attend religious services regularly, their deviant behavior, such as drug use, violence, and delinquency, is reduced.[14]

Better sex lives—A University of Chicago study revealed that those who consistently attend church have a better and more fulfilling sex life than those who don't. Studies by Stanford University showed the same results.[15] (Come on now married folk—this alone should inspire you not to miss church!)

107

How Your Church Wins

The local church is God's house and God's plan. He wants his church to win in every community where it is being built. Part of that winning is that each of us who consider ourselves to be Christ followers are people who can be counted on to be in his house. This consistency helps your home church in several ways:

Momentum—Part of building a thriving local church that touches the community is building a sense of momentum. This type of momentum is built week to week and is largely dependent on your faithfulness. When the church starts experiencing momentum, lives are touched, people are changed, and God's kingdom advances.

A sense of community—The Bible teaches that we are better together. We need each other and we grow together in our faith as we do life together. This happens only when there is consistency. You may think for a moment that you don't need it, but you do. God made you that way. But also you have to realize that people in your church need you. You will affect, encourage, and help people who others may not connect with. The church needs you, and the church wins when you are present.

Teamwork—The local church (and again, the church isn't a building, it's the people) has the greatest calling on the planet: to lead people into a relationship with Jesus Christ. This is our mission; this is our calling. Something this big and this important needs everyone. It needs an all-out team effort. You can't be the kind of team member who expects everyone else to play in the game. You have to do your part, which includes being there each week to welcome new people, to connect to those who are new to church and don't know anyone, to provide energy, hope, and love to everyone who enters the building. You are part of the team, and your team needs you.

Your dependable commitment to the church also means that your pastor wins. Let me take a moment to share something that your pastor may never share with you. At times, being in the ministry can be lonely and difficult. Sometimes pastors feel like they're the only one who is fighting for the church to thrive. People leave the church for some of the silliest reasons and then put it under the umbrella of "We've prayed about it, and God is moving us on." Sometimes pastors take hurtful shots from people. They may come in the form of negative words, behind-the-back gossip, or inappropriate social media posts. The pastor feels called to reach the city and knows that momentum is built Sunday to Sunday, but finds individuals are inconsistent when it comes to God's house. All of this makes the job of your pastor a difficult one. I am not saying your pastor doesn't love you, the city, or the church, or that he or she doesn't find it a joy to be the pastor of the flock you call home. All I am saying is that at times it can be difficult, and inconsistency only adds to a pastor's challenges. Help your pastor: be a friend, be someone who can be counted on, be someone who is dependable each week. Let your pastors feel confident that each time they stand in front and look out into the crowd, you will be there cheering them on. Your church wins when your pastors feel like they are winning, and you can help them have that winning spirit with your week-to-week dependability to the church you call home.

So my final word to you on this chapter is this: *be dependable*. Make church part of your regular weekly life. Attend church, get involved, worship with passion, invite others, welcome new people, smile big, laugh at your pastor's jokes even when they're not funny. Be someone that your pastor, your church family, and, most importantly, your Savior can count on. You will win, and so will the kingdom of God!

Questions for Study and Discussion

1. Where in your life have you shown dependability, and where do you need to start showing more dependability?

2. How have you done with being someone your church family can depend on each week? What have been some of your go-to reasons for why you haven't shown dependability in this area?

3. How might you be an Aaron or Hur in your extended family at church?

six

Quit Your Church Friends

Years ago I had the opportunity to go on a short mission trip to Romania. There I had the chance to see the work of Touched Romania, a ministry founded by Raegan Glugosh, a wonderful friend and outstanding leader. She started this ministry with the primary purpose of rescuing abandoned babies. In Romania, it is fairly common for parents to abandon a baby at the hospital because they cannot afford to raise the child.

The trip was incredible, and I loved seeing all the work that God has done through the ministry Raegan founded. The staff, the mentoring that single moms receive, the homes for those moms who want to raise their child but have no place to go: all of it is absolutely incredible, and you can see the hand of God all over it. One particular part of this ministry stood out. The local hospital has a designated room with ten babies in it. Some of these babies have been completely abandoned, and some are visited in the evening by their parents, who work during the day and are trying to figure out a suitable living situation. One late afternoon, Raegan and a few of her team members took me down to this hospital. As we were approaching the baby room, which they had told me about on the ride over, Raegan stopped me and said, "Chris, there are ten babies in this room. Five of them have been completely abandoned since the day they were born and five of them have parents that visit them in the evening. I want to see if you can tell me which five have been abandoned and which five are being loved by their parents."

We entered the room and I walked around looking at these precious babies. I held a few of them as well. As we finished up our time in the hospital room, she came over to me and said, "Alright, can you tell me which ones have been abandoned and which ones haven't?"

I looked around to the ten small cribs and one by one I pointed at the babies and said "Abandoned" or "Not abandoned." I got every single one right. She asked me, "How did you know?" (She knew exactly how I knew, but she wanted to see if I realized it.)

I told her, "The babies that are not abandoned, when I hold them they make eye contact with me and give me big smiles. The babies that have been abandoned are more lethargic. They don't make eye contact with me. They don't smile. They are very lifeless."

It was one of the saddest and most eye-opening moments that I have ever experienced. I could physically see for the first time the need we have for one another. The babies were only one to two months old. But those who had been abandoned didn't interact with me at all. No smiles, no giggles—nothing. They didn't even make eye contact with me. The babies who were not abandoned were the same age but acted completely different. They were full of life, smiles, small laughs and wouldn't take their eyes off of me. There was only one difference between these babies: one group was receiving consistent affection, love, and attention, and the other was not.

This showed me how much we human beings need each other. We need connection, relationship, and community with each other. It's the way God designed us. In our crazy-busy world, we rarely take the time to connect with others, and as a result we miss out on the fulfillment and satisfaction that only relationships can bring. We actually cut short God's purpose and design for our life when we limit ourselves to shallow and safe-distance relationships.

We make this mistake quite often in our approach to church. It's an interesting dynamic. Someone says to you, "Where do you fellowship?" Then you mention the church you attend. But let's be honest, most of us don't fellowship there—we attend there.

Fellowship doesn't happen when we show up just barely on time for church, hang out in the lobby for a few minutes afterward, head to our cars, drive home, and then do it again the next Sunday. We come to call this group of people that we see in passing once a week our "church friends." But the relationship we have with them can hardly be called "fellowship" in a biblical sense.

These are not the kinds of life-on-life connections we need with each other. God has so much more in mind. We are designed for deep and genuine friendships. The church is meant to be a place of great connection and community with each other.

It's a God Idea

In Genesis 2 we read the story of Adam and Eve. God first created Adam, and then he created Eve. He said, "It is not good for the man to be alone" (v. 18). We might immediately assume this has to do with marriage, but as you search throughout Scripture, you see that God sees it as much more. He designed us to need each other, not just in marriage but in genuine relationship with each other. This isn't just a good idea; it's a God idea. We were created this way.

God created Adam and Eve with the understanding that they were to live in the garden under the umbrella of an intimate relationship with him and with each other, and that their offspring would live this way as well. This was his divine plan. The Creator created us to need each other. Think of it like this. The people who created your car created it in a way that it needs fuel to run. The people who created your appliances at home created them in a way that they need electricity to operate. In both cases, the creator determined what the creation would need. This is how it is with God. He is our Creator, and he created us in such a way that we need connection and relationship with each other.

> The Creator created us to need each other.

Fast-forward to Genesis 6. While this is only four chapters later, sixteen hundred years have passed. God had become upset with humankind. He had created them to be in relationship with him and in relationship with each other. Among other things that displeased God, they were not living the way that he designed. He decided to flood the earth and start over. Let that sink in for a moment. He flooded the earth in part because they were not fulfilling what he had planned for their lives.

God pushes the restart button on the earth with the objective to create a people who would love him and love each other. Years pass, and now the earth is being restored by God with this objective in mind. A few chapters later, in Genesis 12, God introduces the word "tribe." That word gets repeated 445 times throughout the Bible. I think when God says something 445 times, he is trying to make a point. A "tribe" is a group of people who have the same language and beliefs.[16] It's a group of people who love each other, care for each other, serve each other, and do life together. This desire for us as his children to be in close relationship with each other starts in Genesis and carries all the way through Revelation. Chapter after chapter you see his heart as a Father come through. He wants his children to be in relationship with each other. If you're a parent, you get that. You want your children to be close to each other, to have genuine relationship with each other. God as our Father is no different. He wants his children (you and me) to be in close relationship with each other. We see church as a place to attend; he sees church as a place to belong. We weren't meant to have "church friends"; we were meant to have "brothers and sisters," people we do life with.

We Like to Stay Connected but Not Too Connected

All right, time for a little honesty. How many of you live in a state where cell phone use while driving is against the law? But you so desperately want to talk with someone that you use the cell phone while driving (without an earpiece) and are constantly looking in the mirror for a police car? How many of you have ever said "Hold on a minute" to the person you are talking to so you could allow a police car to go by? Or maybe you receive a text while driving. You cannot wait a few more minutes until you arrive at your destination to take a look and respond, even though it might be against the law where you live, and you know it's dangerous.

We have a crazy need to stay connected. But we also avoid being too connected. We want to have relationship with people, but not too much. We want to talk "to" people but not necessarily "with" people. We want to have "church friends" who we say hello to and check in with weekly, but we don't want to have "genuine friends" who we go deep with.

Even though God created you to need these types of relationships, you are probably thinking that you are doing fine without them. That may be true to some extent, but you will never get to a place of complete fulfillment or satisfaction, or ever get all God has for you, until you build the kind of connection he wants his children to have with each other. You are shortchanging yourself and, in a way, shortchanging God of his divine plan and purpose.

Identifying the Roadblocks

Painful Past

You might have been hurt in the past. Maybe it was from a relationship that went sour, or maybe it even happened in the church you used to attend or the one you attend now. Let me start off by saying that I am genuinely sorry that you were hurt. Also, let me say that Jesus sees your pain and knows exactly what you are going through. He had twelve disciples who were close to him, people he did life with. One of them sold him out for money, and one of them, during his time of need, denied knowing him—not once but three times. This rejection Jesus felt created pain in his heart. People who he would call "brother" hurt him. That's why I say he knows exactly how you feel.

You need to seek help to walk through the emotions of this pain. You need to get to the other side of it. I am not saying it will be easy, but you need to do it. You cannot let the pain of your past rob you of the blessing of your future. Your pain doesn't change God's plan for your life: to have genuine relationships with people who are part of your church, people who are part of your spiritual family. These people can serve as part of the healing process. Again, I know it won't be easy to trust again or to allow someone into your life beyond a shallow friendship, but you must work toward it. If you don't, you are allowing those who hurt you to continue hurting you. Don't let them!

Personality

There are many personality tests available. I don't want to get too deep into it, but here is one basic rundown of the four temperaments:

Phlegmatic—Generally quiet. Doesn't like to be the center of attention. Seeks and desires peace. Easy to get along with but has only a few close friends.

Melancholic—Generally more serious. Is more analytical. Can sometimes come across negative. Tends to be reserved and suspicious in forming relationships.

Sanguine—The life of the party. Very social. Enjoys being around people and builds relationships quickly.

Choleric—A natural leader. Loves to be in charge. Sees the need to network, but doesn't see the need for genuine friendships.[17]

Can you see yourself in any of these four personality types? Maybe one doesn't perfectly describe you, but it does in a general sense. Based on your personality type, you might find it easy or hard to build genuine friendships. You might see it as necessary, or, especially if you are choleric, you may not see it as important. Sometimes our personality type can make it difficult to connect with people, either because we are introverted or because we are a natural leader and don't see the need. This is why we "attend" church but never "belong." We never really take time to build the kind of relationships that God desires his people to have with one another. But keep in mind that regardless of your personality type, you are not excused from building community and connection with other believers in your spiritual family. It might mean you need to try a little harder because it doesn't come naturally, but nevertheless you need it, and God's constructed you in a way that you will be better because of it.

Too Busy

We are a crazy-busy society. Work, kids, bills, family, soccer practice, Little League, marriage, house repairs—and the list can literally go on and on. There is so much going on that we simply do not have the time to spend to build community with other believers in our church family. Another night out seems impossible and something you don't want to even try. I get it; I really do. But let me challenge you with a thought. If you are too busy, then you are too busy. If your life is so packed with things that pull you away from God's divine plan for your life, you might need to adjust your lifestyle. Jesus said in John 14:15, "If you love me, show it by doing what I've told you" (Message). Jesus expresses to each of us that if we truly consider ourselves Christ followers, we have to do what he says. Our life is in his hands. Part of doing what he says includes having genuine fellowship with one another: not simply attending church, but belonging; not simply showing up each week, but connecting with those in our church family in a real and authentic way.

So yes, it might require you to adjust your schedule. It might mean you need to say no to some things so you can say yes to the best things. Throughout Scripture, the Lord expresses his desire for us to be a "tribe," to believe in each other, love each other, care for each other, and connect with each other. So if we love him and we call him Lord, we really don't have a choice.

When I talk about "tribe" I can't help but think of Rick and Jeanette. Years ago they were the leaders of a small group at our church. One day a young woman showed up with her two children on Sunday morning, and Rick and Jeanette embraced her and quickly became her friend. The young woman showed up each Sunday to church, but her husband never joined her. She got involved in the small group Rick and Jeanette led and started to build friendships with the other eight to ten people who were part of this group. I'm not sure of all the details, but I know

> The Lord expresses his desire for us to be a "tribe," to believe in each other, love each other, care for each other, and connect with each other.

that after a couple months, this young woman's husband left her and her two children. She was heartbroken and afraid, unsure of what her future held. Over the next few months I watched the small group rally around her. A few of the men in the group rotated doing her yardwork each Saturday, and a few of the women jumped in to help with childcare as she juggled raising her kids and now working a full-time job. I loved watching what was happening. They were being friends. They were being a support base to each other. They were being a tribe. I believe that this display of love put a big smile on God's face. I know it did for me. This was and is God's plan for how he wants us to be with one another.

Your Next Step

The very first official church that was established is described in Acts 2. It was led by the disciples of Jesus after his death and resurrection. The disciples spent more time with Jesus than anyone else, so they knew best what mattered to his heart. That's why they set up the first local church in such a way that the people had genuine and authentic connection with each other. They made it a priority in the church because it was a priority to Jesus. Look at the description of this church:

> They committed themselves to the teaching of the apostles, the life together, the common meal, and the prayers.
> Everyone around was in awe—all those wonders and signs done through the apostles! And all the believers lived in a wonderful harmony, holding everything in common. They sold whatever they owned and pooled their resources so that each person's need was met.

122

They followed a daily discipline of worship in the Temple followed by meals at home, every meal a celebration, exuberant and joyful, as they praised God. (Acts 2:42b–46 Message)

Do you see the description of how the members of this first church interacted with each other? They did life together, ate meals together, met in homes together, pooled resources to help each other, met each other's needs, were joyful in each other's presence, experienced wonderful harmony with each other, and praised God together.

This passage of Scripture about the first church screams the heart of Jesus. He wants his church, his children, to be in genuine and authentic relationship with each other—not just to attend, but to belong. This early church laid out the standard of how our involvement and connection at our churches should be. Doing life with each other, loving each other and building each other up—this goes way past the Sunday "fellowship" that we have for a few minutes in the plaza or lobby following the service. This is about having true intimacy with other believers. And again, I don't see this as an option but as a requirement for those who consider themselves Christ followers.

So what's your next step? Get involved! I am not sure what your church offers. Some churches have small groups, home groups, affinity groups, midweek Bible studies, growth tracks, or some other avenue outside of Sunday morning services. Whatever it is in your church, dive in. Adjust your schedule, rearrange your priorities, and begin to follow Christ in a deeper way by connecting with other believers in your church. Do life with them, build relationships, get connected, follow the model of the first church in Acts 2, and, most importantly, follow the heart of Jesus. He doesn't want you to simply attend; he wants you to belong. Church was never meant to be a weekly event; it was meant to be a body of believers loving each other, caring for each other, serving each other, and changing the world with each other, day in and day out.

Before you start rationalizing all the reasons why this portion of the book isn't for you, *stop*. It is for you. If you have a painful past, it's still for you. If it doesn't quite match your personality, it's still for you. If you are busy, it's still for you. Talk to your pastor or the person in charge of whatever programs your church provides, fill out the card, or go to the info booth and get involved. It's the heart of Jesus, and so it needs to be our heart as well.

> He doesn't want you to simply attend; he wants you to belong.

How You Win

There are so many benefits that come when you decide to move past attending to belonging. God always has a way of rewarding those who obey, blessing those who follow his heart. This subject is no different. When his children take the time and effort to build quality relationships with each other, he, as a loving Father, pours out his favor. Here are a few examples of what you can expect as you take the next step in building relationships with those in your church.

Spiritual Growth

You will find that there is a level of spiritual growth that happens in community. It goes much further than what you can experience on Sunday morning. It allows you a place to grow with each other just like the first church did in Acts 2. They were in the temple (the church) together, but they grew in the Lord outside of the temple, because for them the church didn't start and end on Sunday. Belonging to each other was their life. They were truly the body of Christ, and that body grew better together than it did separately.

Accountability

We do better when we are accountable. That's why people pay money to have a fitness trainer or to belong to a nutrition center, or why they go to a twelve-step program or other sober living communities; we improve ourselves in an environment of accountability. There is no accountability with simply attending church, especially if your church is larger than a couple hundred people. You can easily blend in, and easily stop coming, and most of the time no one will notice. That's why there is such a big benefit for you to be a part of a smaller community in your church: you can have accountability in your life. A home group or Bible study provides you with relationships that will encourage you and keep you on track in your life, marriage, family, and spiritual journey. A smaller group of people will help to make sure you stay focused on what matters most. We all need this.

A Source of Strength during Difficult Times

If you simply attend church, you are not going to have the support base you need when you face difficulty. I always find it interesting that people say, "I was in the hospital and no one came and visited me." I want to say, "The reason no one visited you is most likely because no one knows you."

125

If you want friends, you have to be a friend. If you want a support base of people, you have to step out and become part of a group. That way, when you are in the hospital, facing a tragedy, or going through a difficult time, you have people who are surrounding you with prayer and support.

Lots of benefits are there for those who are willing to step out and get plugged in, for those willing to not simply attend but to belong. So find your place at your church and dive in. You will get so much out of it!

How Your Church Wins

The benefits of deciding to take the next step in your spiritual journey and get deeply connected to the body of Christ go beyond just yourself; they overflow into the life of your church. When you dive in, the church wins. Here are some examples of how that happens.

As we've discussed in earlier chapters, God wants his church to grow. He wants more people to be reached. But a bigger church can often seem impersonal. When you get involved beyond Sunday morning, you are becoming part of the solution. You are helping your church stay true to the intimacy that a small church can provide, while at the same time allowing it to grow. That's the objective of a church: to be growing and reaching people but to still be providing the intimacy and closeness that God desires for us to have. Your church wins when you step out.

"Culture" is a certain set of behaviors.[18] Every church has a set culture or pattern of behaviors that they follow. The culture could include generosity, friendliness, compassion, outreach-mindedness, and so on. Whatever the set culture of the church is, the majority of people will follow. As new people come in to the church, they too will adapt to the culture that has been set. If being connected beyond Sunday morning and having true community with each other is part of the culture of your church, then that's what people will naturally do as the church grows. As the culture goes, so go the people. Any growing and healthy church wants a good culture. They want the people to be connected to each other outside of Sunday morning. So when you decide to step out of your comfort zone and get connected, you are helping to set a healthy, life-giving, and God-honoring culture that others will follow.

The Challenge

So here's my challenge to you. Find a place in your church to get connected beyond Sunday morning, and dive in. It might be small groups, life groups, Bible studies, growth tracks, or something else that is provided by your church. Whatever it is, get plugged in. Don't allow yourself to make excuses. We are all busy and have plenty going on, but we always make time for what's important. And to Jesus, this is important.

You might say it's not in your personality, but as I said earlier, regardless of your personality, it is what God desires for you. He has designed you in such a way that you will experience great joy and satisfaction if you would simply get connected. Today is your day. Get connected. Build relationships. Do life with those in your church. Follow the heart of God on this. Follow the example of the first church. It may be a little out of your comfort zone at first, and quite honestly it might be a bit of a hassle, but I am completely confident that in the end you will be glad you did.

Questions for Study and Discussion

1. What do you struggle with the most in building relationships/friendships?

2. How many relationships do you have with others in your church?

3. How can you be more effective relationally in your church body?

4. Can you see the difference in your life when you're in healthy relationships in the church versus when you're not?

5. What step can you commit to right now to have healthier and stronger relationships with people in your church family?

CONCLUSION

It's Quitting Time

Let me take you back to the first chapter, where we learned that quitting wasn't the problem, it was the solution. Any time you want to succeed, there is always something you will have to give up. That's the way success works. It's about the trade-offs you are willing to make. From fitness to finances, if you want to see change, you have to be willing to quit something. You can't keep doing the same things and expect different results. When it comes to your spiritual journey, there is a God in heaven who is crazy in love with you. He desires to give you so much. He is ready to shower you with his favor and blessing. However, as we have learned throughout this book, there are things you are going to have to quit. There is a casual approach to some of the spiritual behaviors that need to change in your life. Once you take a different approach, God releases so much new blessing on our life. It's simple: Do you want everything that God has for you? Do you want all that sits in his treasure chest, the one that has your name on it? If so, then you have to quit. Once you decide to quit any area that you have been giving a half-hearted effort to and start to fully engage in his plan and direction, God begins to meet you with new and exciting rewards that he has been waiting to pour out.

When you quit, you win.

There's another amazing reward that comes to those who quit: the freedom to finally let go of something that has been holding you down. This book is all about helping you realize that there are negative attitudes and behaviors that keep you from reaching all that God has for your life, and helping you come to the knowledge that these attitudes and behaviors have been holding you down for way too long and that you need to let them go once and for all. You need to give them up. You need to be set free from them. In short, you need to quit. Like a balloon that was meant to soar, you are being held down with a weight, and once you cut the string by changing your attitude and behavior toward the things addressed in this book, you will start to soar. You will be free. Your potential awaits you.

I also love that quitting means the local church wins. When I say the local church, I mean your church. Imagine with me for a moment that every person in your church (including you) decided to quit, to give up any casual approach they've had to the areas we have discussed in the previous chapters. Can you imagine what your church would accomplish, the eternal difference you could make together, the impact you could have in your community? Together, your church could begin to do things that you could never do by yourself.

130

Imagine with Me . . .

What if everyone in your church was completely loyal to the pastor, the leadership, and the church? No gossip, no back talk, no critical spirit. Just loving each other and believing the best.

What if everyone in your church started to honor God by regularly giving a healthy percentage of their income? Can you imagine the number of people that could be reached, the global impact your church could have, the help your church could provide to those in need? It's astounding!

What if everyone in your church started to serve, to get involved, to utilize their talents and gifts for the cause of the kingdom of God? There is so much more that could be done if we all did our part!

What if everyone in your church truly reached out and invited those far from God? You would see a church filled each Sunday with unchurched people who are there to discover the love of Jesus for the first time in their lives. The biggest problem your church would have would be finding enough seats!

> When we quit our casual approach to the areas we've discussed and begin to engage at a new level, God pours out his blessing on us and on our church.

Can you see it? Can you grab hold of what this could look like? It's a crazy formula that God has created. When we quit our casual approach to the areas we've discussed and begin to engage at a new level, God pours out his blessing on us and on our church. What an opportunity! What an incredible God we serve! We follow what he says and everybody wins!

I have been teaching this concept at conferences, seminars, and churches across the nation, and I have seen and heard firsthand the results of those who have quit, those who made a decision to fully engage in all that God wants from them and for them. I started keeping a log of the stories I have heard from people who made the decision to quit. These stories are from people just like you, people who heard the message and responded, and then the Lord did his part. If it happened for them, it can and will happen for you.

Stories from Some Amazing Quitters

Rick and Cyndi are a young couple who have been attending their midwestern church for a few years but always remained on the sidelines. They would hear about the small groups that their church offered and would often say they would start attending, but they never did. They admitted that they felt that they were just too busy, and Rick said, "It just wasn't my cup of tea." Then they decided to quit making excuses and take the plunge. They signed up for a small group and started attending. At first it was a little awkward for them, and sometimes due to their schedules it was difficult to attend. But they stuck it out. They have now been part of the group for almost two years and absolutely love it. They feel that they have grown spiritually as a result and have built some amazing friendships. They feel like they are no longer doing Christianity alone but are on the journey with others. In their words, "We don't know why we waited so long, but we will never stop being a part of groups outside of Sunday. We are better and our church is better because of it."

132

Tyler and Stephanie have two small children and have been attending their church for almost three years. They were attending faithfully but never offered to volunteer in any area of ministry. They just always felt like someone else would take care of it, and with two small children it just didn't seem to work out in their schedule. One day they decided to quit, to stop using these reasons for not serving, and to start to do their part. So they signed up to be a part of the greeting team at the church. They said it was kind of strange at first, because they had never volunteered before. But after a while they loved it. They said, "We feel like we are making a difference. Each time we serve, we get the privilege of giving a warm smile or friendly hug to someone who maybe hasn't received that kind of love all week long. We now feel like we are playing our part in the church and feel absolutely blessed to do it."

Jose and Carla grew up in church. Each week their parents would take them to Mass. After getting married, they started attending a Protestant church just a few blocks from their home. They were faithful to attend, serve, and give each and every week. They never viewed reaching out to their friends, neighbors, and coworkers as their responsibility. They thought that it was the pastor's responsibility to get new people in the church. After attending a funeral for someone they had known but never shared their faith with, they decided on the drive home that they would quit—no more thinking it was the pastor's job and not their spiritual responsibility. So they started inviting friends and family. They weren't pushy; they just gently shared their faith and pointed the way. As a result, in a twelve-month period they connected six new people to their church, and two of them are now serving and one of them recently was baptized.

Thomas and Athena have been married for over fifteen years and have been attending the small church in their community for the past four years. They struggled financially for most of their marriage and, by their own admission, have made some bad financial choices. The idea of tithing seemed impossible due to the debt caused by their past choices to live above their means. In addition, Thomas had always had the attitude that the church is all about money. After hearing a message about God's plan for their finances and, quite honestly, after years of being frustrated with their situation, they finally decided to quit—to give up their way of running their finances and to quit judging their church by thinking it's all about money. They started tithing immediately. In their own words, "We didn't know how we were going to make it, but we knew we needed to trust Jesus." Simultaneously, they started getting financial guidance. It's now been almost two and a half years since they started this journey, and they said, "It was the best choice we ever made." They expressed, "We have never missed giving our tithe, yet somehow were able to pay our bills. We don't know how God does it, but he does. We love his math." In addition, they just finished paying off their last credit card and are now completely out of debt.

Jason and Jill's story is a little different. They have been married for almost twenty years, and in that time have attended six different churches. They always had a way of finding a problem with the pastor, someone in leadership, a decision that was made, or something about the Sunday service. One way or another, they would find a new church, and then, within two or three years, find the problems and leave the church. Unfortunately, in a couple of incidents they said things they shouldn't have said to people they shouldn't have said them to. As a result, people got hurt. One day while they were sitting in church, the Spirit of God worked on their hearts like only he can. They recognized the critical and judgmental spirit they had had and the damage they had caused. They spoke to each other and decided to quit on that very Sunday: no more being critical and always looking for faults; no more being the problem or pointing out the problem. Instead, they would be a positive solution in their church. They even went to a few of the pastors and leaders they had hurt in the past and asked for forgiveness. They are now fully engaged in the church they attend and are some of the most positive and supportive people you would ever meet. What an amazing story of life change! They did what most people don't do. They looked in the mirror and said, "Maybe it's me. Maybe I'm the problem."

Now It's Your Turn

These are just a few of the many stories I've heard about people who chose to quit. I'm not the only one that has these stories. Your pastors do too. They've seen what happens when people step out in obedience to the spiritual practices God calls us to. It reminds me of the story of Jesus and Peter in Matthew 14. Peter and the other disciples were crossing the lake early in the morning when they saw Jesus coming toward them, walking on the water. Peter had the guts to ask if he could come out on the water too. I'm also reminded of the bold shepherd boy known as David, and how his older brothers cowered before Goliath. Then David, knowing God

135

would be with him, told his brothers that he would be the one to fight. He would step out in faith.

The Bible is filled with examples of men and women who trusted the Lord their God and stepped out when others stepped back. In each story, we see the faithfulness of God. And now thousands of years later that same God is faithful to those individuals whose stories you just read, and he will be faithful to you as well. Today is your day. Today it is your turn to step out in faith and see for yourself the miracle-working hand of God all over your life.

Let me close out this book by asking two potentially life-changing questions.

What Do You Need to Quit?

When my daughter was nine or ten years old, she had a problem with complaining. She had a bad attitude toward her younger brother. She complained if we asked her to pick up her room. She griped and moaned anytime for anything. So I came up with an idea. I took a big plastic jar and put a small sign on it that said "Complaining Jar." I told my wife and two kids that anyone caught with a bad attitude or complaining about something would have to put one dollar in the jar. For my kids, who were only getting a few dollars a week for chores around the house, this was a significant amount of money. Over the next couple of weeks, every time I heard my daughter complaining, I said, "Grace, are you complaining?" and she would

> Today it is your turn to step out in faith and see for yourself the miracle-working hand of God all over your life.

quickly say, "No, Daddy, I'm not complaining." This went on for a couple weeks. Every time I caught her complaining, she would immediately stop at the threat of losing a dollar. One day, however, she was really upset about something. I said, "Grace, are you complaining?"

She said in a strong voice, "Yes, I am."

I said "OK, then you have to go get a dollar and put it in the jar."

She stomped her way upstairs, fiddled through her piggy bank, and charged back downstairs. She aggressively made her way to the complaining jar and said, "Here's a dollar for now, and here's one for later. I'm not done."

It took everything in me not to laugh out loud. But I was trying desperately to teach my young daughter an important lesson. Complaining and a bad attitude won't get you anywhere. I wanted her to quit doing it, because I knew how damaging it can be, and I also knew how rewarding and beneficial a winning spirit can be.

So my question to you is, What do you need to quit? You've read the book. You've learned of the spiritual practices God wants from you. You've heard the stories and seen how Scripture promises what God does when you do your part. So now it's your turn to quit. It's your turn to identify the area where you need to stop making excuses, putting it off, or pretending it somehow doesn't apply to you.

Below are six statements, one for each spiritual practice that I have challenged you with through this book. Read through these statements, and mark any that describe you. Maybe they won't perfectly describe you, but if you're honest, there may be some truth about you in one or more of these six statements.

☐ Sometimes I can be critical of my pastor and leadership team. I often judge their motives, and at times I speak poorly of them. I don't pray for or support them in the way God would want me to. I need to quit it.

☐ I don't tithe as I should. I find it hard to trust Jesus with my finances. At times I think the church is all about money or that I can't afford it. I have all sorts of reasons to not follow God in this area, but I know I need to. I need to quit thinking this way.

☐ I realize that there are lots of areas to serve and volunteer in, but I don't have the time. I figure that there are other people who can help out, and that serving is just not my thing. It's a wrong mind-set and wrong perspective, and I need to quit it.

☐ Sometimes I might invite someone to church, but not too often. I don't really invest in my friends, family, coworkers, and neighbors. I don't pray for them to find Christ, either. I find bringing up the subject un-comfortable, or I just don't think about it in my day. But people need the Lord, and I have a responsibility. I need to quit it.

☐ It's easier for me to find reasons not to go to church each Sunday. There's always something to do or somewhere to be. I'm not faithful and consistent when it comes to being in God's house each week, and that needs to change. I need to quit.

☐ I go to church, I often give, and sometimes I even volun-teer, but beyond my Sunday appearance, I am not really connected to others. The extent of my relationship with people is just a few minutes in the lobby after the service.

I don't have relationships with people through the programs my church provides, such as small groups or Bible
studies. I attend, but I don't belong. I need to quit.

If you find any truth about yourself in any or all of these
statements, the first decision you have to make is to quit,
to decide right now, "I am not going to be that person anymore. I am going to quit." If you don't, you will be missing
out on so much. You will keep yourself from winning at
new levels, and you will keep your church (God's church)
from winning at new levels. There is way too much at stake,
way too much to gain, way too many rewards and blessings
for you to leave on the table simply because you won't quit.

What Do You Need to Start?

James 1:22 instructs us this way: "Don't fool yourself into
thinking that you are a listener when you are anything but,
letting the Word go in one ear and out the other. Act on what
you hear!" (Message). The Word of God isn't simply something to read; it is something to do. The spiritual practices
that we have gone over in this book are meant to be put into
action. It is our action that releases God's hand all over our
life and all over the church we call home.

Think of it like a set of keys. Each of these keys opens
up great opportunity and blessing. However, unless you
use the keys, they don't open up anything for your life or
for your spiritual family, the church. So that raises some
questions: What are you going to do about this? What are
you going to start doing that you haven't been doing faithfully in the past?

Once you have figured those things out and you've come to realize what you need to start doing, you need to take action, and you need to take it immediately. Here are a few things you can do to ensure that you are a doer of the Word and not just a hearer:

Tell someone close to you—Let a person who loves you and will hold you accountable know about the next steps you are taking. Be honest with them about what has happened in your life that brought you to this decision.

Tell your pastor or leader—Find a spiritual leader in your church. Tell them what you are going to quit and what you are going to start. If you belong to a home group or small group, let them know of your decision.

Never wait for the right time, because the right time is now—Ecclesiastes 11:4 gives us a warning: "If you wait for perfect conditions, you will never get anything done" (TLB). You can't wait for things to be perfect before you get involved. Start building relationships, start giving, start inviting the unchurched. If you wait until things are perfect, you will never get anything done. Start now, and trust Jesus in the process. He won't let you down!

Do This for You

My prayer for you is that you will learn to quit; that you will learn to stop doing, thinking, or behaving in the ways that go against the spiritual practices that God desires for you; that you will realize how much he loves you and how much he wants to bless your life. You hold the keys. It's your decision, and I am praying that you make the right one. Put these practices into action, and watch how the Lord will be true to his Word.

Do This for Your Church

Your church will win when you decide to quit. Your church will experience a new level of success as you step out and do what God has called you to do. Your pastor needs you, your leadership needs you, and your spiritual family needs you. They are counting on you. Remember what we learned earlier: personal choices are never personal. If you don't take action, it won't affect just you; it will affect many others as well. Being a part of a spiritual family means there are family responsibilities. Do your part, and watch what happens.

Do This for Jesus

Jesus is crazy about you. He loves you and is cheering you on. He is leaning in to see how you are going to respond to this challenge. You are his child. He wants you to win. No doubt he will bless and reward you as you step out, but I challenge you to do this for Jesus simply because you love him. Do this not because of what he will do for you (and he will) but because he is the Lord of your life, the Master of your soul, the strength when you are weak, the hope when you feel hopeless, the rock when you feel unstable, and the shield when difficulty surrounds you. Do it simply because of who he is, not because of what he can and will do.

Do This Now

Put quitting into practice. Watch how you'll win. Watch how your church will win. You were created for great things in Jesus, and now is your time. Now is the moment for you to rise up and shout out to everyone around you these life-changing words: "*I quit!*"

Questions for Study and Discussion

Below are the six statements that were listed in this chapter, one statement for each spiritual practice that we've been challenged to change. Which of these statements resonate with you the most, and why? What can you do to quit? How can you make a change in these areas?

☐ Sometimes I can be critical of my pastor and leadership team. I often judge their motives, and at times I speak poorly of them. I don't pray for or support them in the way God would want me to. I need to quit it.

☐ I don't tithe as I should. I find it hard to trust Jesus with my finances. At times I think the church is all about money or that I can't afford it. I have all sorts of reasons to not follow God in this area but I know I need to. I need to quit thinking this way.

☐ I realize that there are lots of areas to serve and volunteer in, but I don't have the time. I figure that there are other people who can help out and that serving is just not my thing. It's a wrong mind-set and wrong perspective, and I need to quit it.

☐ Sometimes I might invite someone to church, but not too often. I don't really invest in my friends, family, coworkers, and neighbors. I don't pray for them to find Christ, either. I find bringing up the subject uncomfortable, or I just don't think about it in my day. But people need the Lord, and I have a responsibility. I need to quit it.

☐ It's easier for me to find reasons not to go to church each Sunday. There's always something to do or somewhere to be. I'm not faithful and consistent when it comes

143

to being in God's house each week, and that needs to change. I need to quit.

☐ I go to church, I often give, and sometimes I even volunteer, but beyond my Sunday appearance, I am not really connected to others. The extent of my relationship with people is just a few minutes in the lobby after the service. I don't have relationships with people through the programs my church provides, such as small groups or Bible studies. I attend, but I don't belong. I need to quit.

NOTES

1. Mike Holmes, "What Would Happen If the Church Tithed?," *Relevant*, March 8, 2016, https://relevantmagazine.com/god/church/what -would-happen-if-church-tithed.

2. "Is Evangelism Going Out of Style?," Barna, December 17, 2013, https://www.barna.com/research/is-evangelism-going-out-of-style/.

3. Holmes, "What Would Happen."

4. Holmes, "What Would Happen"; Keith Edwards, "Tithing, a Timeless Principle of Discipleship" (sermon, Centerpointe Church, Fairfax, VA, June 25, 2017), http://centerpointechurch.com/messages/tithing -timeless-principle-discipleship/.

5. "In Memory of George Ferdinand Muller," GeorgeMuller.org, July 5, 2016, http://www.georgemuller.org/devotional/in-memory-of-george -ferdinand-muller.

6. Michael Corkery and Stacy Cowley, "Household Debt Makes a Comeback in the U.S.," *New York Times*, May 17, 2017, https://www .nytimes.com/2017/05/17/business/dealbook/household-debt-united -states.html.

7. Erin El Issa, "2016 American Household Credit Card Debt Study," Nerdwallet, accessed November 1, 2017, https://www.nerdwallet.com /blog/average-credit-card-debt-household/.

8. Claire Shinn, "8 Long-Term Health Benefits of Volunteering," Nonprofit Hub, accessed November 1, 2017, http://nonprofithub.org/featured /8-long-term-health-benefits-of-volunteering/.

9. Bill Hybels, "Closing Message," Willow Creek Association Global Leadership Summit, August 10, 2012. See Tim Peters, *The Global Leadership Summit: Summit Summary*, p. 44, https://www.willowcreek

.com/topshelf/images/newSummit_ebook_sm.pdf; Matt Perman, "Bill Hybels—The Local Church Is the Hope of the World," What's Best Next, August 10, 2012, https://www.whatsbestnext.com/2012/08/bill-hybels -the-local-church-is-the-hope-of-the-world/.

10. Thom S. Rainer, "Ten Surprises about the Unchurched," *Christianity Today*, accessed November 1, 2017, http://www.christianitytoday .com/pastors/2007/july-online-only/102704.html.

11. Thom S. Rainer, "The Number One Reason for the Decline in Church Attendance and Five Ways to Address It," Thom Rainer (website), August 19, 2013, http://thomrainer.com/2013/08/the-number-one-reason -for-the-decline-in-church-attendance-and-five-ways-to-address-it/.

12. Vern Bengtson, "Religion Runs in the Family," interview by Amy Ziettlow, *Christianity Today*, September 20, 2013, http://www.christian itytoday.com/ct/2013/august-web-only/religion-runs-in-family.html.

13. Shanshan Li et al., "Association of Religious Service Attendance with Mortality among Women," *JAMA Internal Medicine* 176, no. 6 (June 2016): 777–85, https://doi.org/10.1001/jamainternmed.2016.1615; cited in Carina Storrs, "Going to Church Could Help You Live Longer, Study Says," CNN, May 16, 2016, http://www.cnn.com/2016/05/16/health /religion-lifespan-health/index.html.

14. Patrick Fagan, "Why Religion Matters Even More: The Impact of Religious Practice on Social Stability," The Heritage Foundation, December 18, 2006, http://www.heritage.org/.

15. Research cited and summarized in Peter Haas, "The Jaw Dropping Benefits of Church Attendance," PeterHaas.org, August 19, 2014, https:// www.peterhaas.org/the-jaw-dropping-benefits-of-church-attendance/.

16. See *Merriam-Webster Unabridged*, s.v. "tribe," accessed November 6, 2017, http://unabridged.merriam-webster.com/unabridged/tribe.

17. "The Four Primary Temperaments," The Four Temperaments (website), accessed November 1, 2017, http://fourtemperaments.com /4-primary-temperaments/.

18. See David Matsumoto, "Culture, Context, and Behavior," *Journal of Personality* 75, no. 6 (December 2007): 1293, https://doi.org/10.1111 /j.1467-6494.2007.00476.x.

Chris Sonksen understands church growth and how to help pastors who may feel stuck because their church isn't growing. His personal experience comes from his own success in pioneering South Hills Church, a multicampus church that has been widely recognized for its unprecedented growth and strategic approaches to doing ministry. In addition, Chris's church-growth expertise led him to found Church BOOM, an organization that has provided personal coaching to thousands of leaders. Chris and his wife, Laura, have two children and live in Southern California.

CONNECT WITH CHRIS!

To learn more about his ministry, speaking
engagements, and leadership, visit

ChrisSonksen.com

 ChrisSonksen

 ChrisSonksen

 ChrisSonksen

"A guide to reignite your church's growth."

—ANDY STANLEY, senior pastor at North Point Ministries

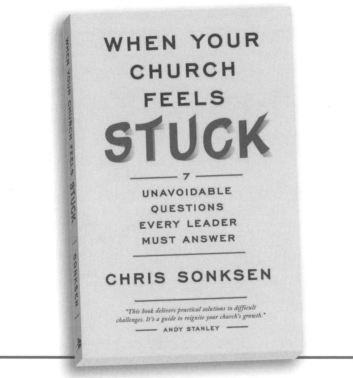

When Your Church Feels Stuck poses seven unavoidable questions church leaders must answer before they can chart the unique path to growth for their church. These challenging questions address the key subjects of mission, strategy, values, metrics, team alignment, culture, and services, and the way you and your team answer these questions will help you discover the real reasons your church is stuck—and what steps you need to take in order to facilitate real growth.

CHURCH BOOM

LEADING A CHURCH IS HARD. WE MAKE IT EASIER.

Church BOOM's team of successful, seasoned pastors wants to help you face and overcome the obstacles keeping you from experiencing explosive growth in your church.

- Personal Coaching Call Opportunities
- Video Training Modules
- Full Library of Downloadable Resources
- Complete Sermon Series Branding Packages

WE BELIEVE THAT CHURCH
ISN'T JUST A PLACE TO ATTEND,
BUT RATHER A COMMUNITY WE
CAN BELONG TO. OUR VISION IS
TO LEAD UNCHURCHED PEOPLE
INTO GROWING RELATIONSHIPS
WITH JESUS CHRIST.

www.SouthHills.org